Teaching, Occupational and Further Education

Sai Loo

Teaching, Occupational and Further Education

Pedagogy, Identities and Knowledge

 Springer

Sai Loo
UCL's Faculty of Education and Society
Institute of Education
University College London
London, UK

ISBN 978-3-031-67290-3   ISBN 978-3-031-67291-0 (eBook)
https://doi.org/10.1007/978-3-031-67291-0

© The Editor(s) (if applicable) and The Author(s), under exclusive license to Springer Nature Switzerland AG 2024

This work is subject to copyright. All rights are solely and exclusively licensed by the Publisher, whether the whole or part of the material is concerned, specifically the rights of translation, reprinting, reuse of illustrations, recitation, broadcasting, reproduction on microfilms or in any other physical way, and transmission or information storage and retrieval, electronic adaptation, computer software, or by similar or dissimilar methodology now known or hereafter developed.
The use of general descriptive names, registered names, trademarks, service marks, etc. in this publication does not imply, even in the absence of a specific statement, that such names are exempt from the relevant protective laws and regulations and therefore free for general use.
The publisher, the authors and the editors are safe to assume that the advice and information in this book are believed to be true and accurate at the date of publication. Neither the publisher nor the authors or the editors give a warranty, expressed or implied, with respect to the material contained herein or for any errors or omissions that may have been made. The publisher remains neutral with regard to jurisdictional claims in published maps and institutional affiliations.

This Springer imprint is published by the registered company Springer Nature Switzerland AG
The registered company address is: Gewerbestrasse 11, 6330 Cham, Switzerland

If disposing of this product, please recycle the paper.

Swim against the tide and achieve whatever we can in our chosen field. Fate dictated that mine was that of theatre and, within that, I have a responsibility to be as positive and creative as I can. To give way to despair is the ultimate cop-out.

Peter Brook (1925–2022)

In memory of my father.

To Caroline and Anna for their continuing patience and encouragement. And not forgetting Tosca, who is sadly missed.

Acknowledgements

My thanks to Claudia Acuna and Astrid Noordermeer, editors at Springer, for taking on this under-researched and new area of education—occupational education—and having the trust and vision to enable me to bring this book to completion. Lastly, the unsung heroes—the book proposal reviewers—who kindly reviewed the initial book proposal and the submitted manuscript with insightful and supportive comments.

Contents

1	**Prologue**	1
	Introduction and the Further Education (FE) Sector	1
	Scope and Aims	3
	Contents	4
	References	5
2	**An Epistemological Approach of Occupational/Vocational and Academic Subject Pedagogies from Teaching Perspective: Coda to the Conceptual Framework of the Occupational Pedagogy of Teachers: Mark II**	7
	Introduction	8
	Literature Review and the Conceptual Framework	13
	Teaching Practice	17
	Occupational Practice	19
	Research Project	20
	Discussion	21
	Clarification of Misunderstandings	21
	Further Development of TVET and Academic Subject Pedagogies and Intellectual Space for Identity Formation	23
	Inclusion of Two Further Implementation Approaches: 'Signature Pedagogies' (Shulman 2005) and 'Logic of Practice' (Bourdieu 1992)	26
	Conclusion	28
	References	29
3	**A Comparison of Occupational Education of Teacher Educators' Knowledge and Pedagogy**	33
	Introduction	33
	Review of Relevant Literature Sources	34
	Project Details	41

	Findings	42
	FE Colleges	42
	Universities	44
	Private Providers	46
	Discussion	47
	Theoretical Framework	47
	Commonalities and Differences Across the Three Sectors	49
	Conclusion	53
	References	53
4	**A Comparison of TVET Teachers and Teacher Educators' Professional Identities**	57
	Introduction	57
	Relevant Literature Sources	58
	Project Details	63
	Findings and Discussion	64
	Similarities	64
	Differences	68
	Conclusion	70
	References	70
5	**A Systematic Review of Literature of Teacher Educators' Knowledge**	73
	Introduction	73
	Methodological Approach	75
	Findings and Discussion	114
	Part 1—Analysis of the 52 Literature Sources	114
	Part 2—Answering the Two Research Questions	118
	Conclusion	121
	References	121
6	**Epilogue**	125
	Introduction	125
	Re-cap of the Monograph	126
	Implications and Applications	127
	Conclusion and Directions for Further Research	130
	References	131

About the Author

Dr. Sai Loo (Ph.D., MA, B.Sc., FHEA, ACA, FETC) is an academic at the Institute of Education, UCL's Faculty of Education and Society, University College London, and an author and editor of research monographs. Before joining UCL, he taught accounting and finance at higher education institutions in undergraduate, postgraduate, and professional programmes and vocational areas in further education. Before becoming a teacher, Sai worked as a Chartered Accountant in the industry. He has created Occupational Education (OE) as a new area of education and is his main area of expertise and research interest. He takes an interdisciplinary approach to vocationally oriented education of work, teaching and learning settings. His research projects and publications have focused on the further and higher education sectors and professional education, especially around teacher education (teacher educators and teachers) and professional practices in work-related settings of the digital economy and clinical disciplines. He has published widely in over 160 publications, conference papers, and keynotes (80 per cent are single authored). *Teaching, Occupational and Further Education—Pedagogy, Identities and Knowledge* published by Springer, is his ninth research monograph.

List of Figures

Fig. 2.1 A conceptual framework of the occupational pedagogy of teachers (mark I) 14
Fig. 2.2 A conceptual framework of the occupational pedagogy of teachers (mark II) 24
Fig. 3.1 A conceptual framework of (further education) teacher educators' (TE) pedagogic activities 38

Chapter 1
Prologue

Abstract This chapter introduces the scope and aims of this monograph, a collection of standalone contributions. The description of the further education (FE) sector sets the contexts in England, especially the prevalence and importance of vocational education. Vocational education has been lamentably lacking in discussions on the FE sector. It will also explain and delineate the connection with a broader concept of occupational education (OE), which I have created to encompass the FE sector, higher education, and professional education. OE is a new research area in education that intersects work, teaching, and learning. The chapter will introduce the four book chapters, and a final one will bring this introductory chapter to a close.

Keywords Introduction · Scope and aims · Further education (FE) sector · England · Vocational education and training (VET) · Occupational education (OE)

Introduction and the Further Education (FE) Sector

This research monograph aims to offer interested readers deep insights into how lecturers and teacher educators perform as educationists. These performative actions cover their know-how, pedagogic agencies, and identities. Know-how may be viewed broadly to encompass knowledge (e.g., disciplinary, pedagogic, explicit, implicit), experiences, capabilities/abilities, and skillsets. Loo's research monographs (2018, 2019) offer detailed discussions of FE lecturers' know-how. For delineations of the further education (FE) teacher educators' know-how, please refer to Loo's (2020) monograph.

Its scope relates to the FE sector in England. FE occupies a porous ecology with the two compulsory education sectors of primary and secondary on the one side and the higher education sector and professional education on the other. The sector is porous because its pedagogic activities overlap those of the different sectors on either side of FE. This in-betweenness is exemplified by the similarities in teaching, such as work-related courses in the secondary, higher and professional sectors. There are also FE institutions that offer university-level programmes in partnership with connected

HE institutions as accreditation bodies. These university-level courses may be at Level 5 and above based on the European qualifications framework (EQF), where the university level starts at Level 5.

FE, historically, acts as an inclusive and widening participatory role to further former compulsory learners' lifelong learning aims. These aims include both academic and vocational studies.

The diversity of its institutions complements the porosity and inclusivity of FE. "FE providers include any institutions or organisations (other than schools or universities) that receive government funding to provide education and training to people over the age of 16 (some also offer courses for 14 and 15-year-olds). There are six types of FE provider: colleges, Independent Training Providers (ITPs), Local Authority (LA) providers, employer providers, third sector providers, and Adult Community Education (ACE) providers" (Education Training Foundation no date). The largest provider is the General Further Education (GFE) Colleges with 169 colleges (67%) and the next biggest provider, 61 Sixth Form colleges (23%) out of 266 colleges in England. Vocational qualification includes Higher National Certificates /Diplomas, Technical Certificates, Technical Levels, Applied Generals, Branded Vocational Qualifications (e.g., Business and Technology Education Council (BTECs)), T Levels, Foundation Degrees, and Postgraduate Certification of Education (PGCE). Academic qualifications include General Certification of Secondary Education (GCSEs), A, AS Levels and International Baccalaureate (IB) Diplomas (ETF no date).

The extent of this diversity included 2.2 million learners in 2019, of which 1.4 million were adults, 685,000 were 16- to 18-year-olds, and 76,000 were 16- to 18-year-olds who undertook apprenticeships (Association of Colleges 2019). The vocational nature of the sector is further highlighted by the fact that 73.2% of its teaching staff teach in occupational/vocational programmes. The largest five areas: health, public services, and care (11.2%) arts, media and publishing (10.7%), preparation for life and work (9.7%), engineering and manufacturing technologies (8.9%) and construction, planning and the built environment making 48.0% of the total offers in the sector (Frontier Economics 2020, Fig. 54). These courses in FE are known as vocational education and training.

The above evidence highlights the porosity, inclusivity, and diversity of this sector. Because of these characteristics, the FE sector is the least understood of the education sectors. Additionally, it has a variety of voices. The other significant sociocultural factor relates to the preponderance of work-related programme offers, which are considered second to the academic ones. This 'English context' needs to be considered when investigating the FE sector (Loo and Jameson 2017). Social justice underpins these four characteristics. Lastly, FE institutions are classified in the public sector with extended powers in the Skills and Post-16 Education Act 2022. This approach by the current Conservative government is a complete reversal of the Further and Higher Education Act 1992. The implications of this 180 degrees turnaround may be too early to evaluate. However, more bureaucracy and red tape are envisaged (FE News 2022).

Scope and Aims

The approach of this book, a collection of standalone contributions, is to provide four perspectives on the FE sector. These perspectives come in the form of chapters that deal with some of the characteristics of FE. They include occupational/vocational elements, especially related courses, teaching staff know-how, pedagogic approaches, and identities. Complementing these four standalone chapters are the chapters introducing them and a final one that offers overviews. Thus, this monograph is about the performative agencies of lecturers and teacher educators in the FE sector.

I believe and argue that the sector has been overlooked and misunderstood by policymakers because of its porous, inclusive, diverse, and prominent features of vocational offers. It also does not help, not to have one coherent voice. To rectify this misconception and re-emphasize the importance of this sector in the English educational ecology, I would like to re-frame FE as a rich, all-encompassing, and connected sector (with other sectors). People of all abilities and varieties have the educational opportunities to better themselves as lifelong learners irrespective of their age, ethnicity, gender, disabilities, station in life, etc. FE should be re-envisioned as more amoebic space of education, which differs from schools, universities and private providers' tighter specifications of tasks, priorities, and outcomes. This amoebic social space is constituted by many voices, expectations, and the way these narratives create stories-so-far. This epistemology is supported by the sector's characteristics (such as porosity, inclusivity, diversity with vocational offers) as discussed in the opening section.[1]

To do this, we need to re-imagine work-related education and training not as a second-best alternative to academic education, but like in Germany, on par with its academic relative. We need to have a new language of educational engagement by calling vocational education and training a new and more encompassing term: occupational education (OE). The conventional notion of divide and rule has shown not to work in our highly socio-culturally bound society. OE intersects work, teaching and learning across pre-university (or vocational), higher education (higher vocational), and professional education. It also accords with lifelong learning across all ages and from education to work settings. OE also connects vocational, technical vocational education and training (TVET), higher vocational, and professional education, dissolving such sub-sets in this socially divisive typology. A lengthier delineation of this term is available in Loo (2018, 2019) and Loo and Sutton (2021). It also needs to be pointed out that TVET (or vocational education and training (VET) in England) in other countries has its educational pathway complementing the academic route and not necessarily a pathway into higher education.

---

[1] I am grateful to the Reviewer's suggestion.

Contents

Concerning the contents of this monograph, the standalone chapters reflect the prominence occupational education plays in FE. After the opening chapter—Prologue—that introduces the approach of this book, the second chapter develops the theoretical framework of the occupational pedagogy of FE teachers (Loo 2018). These relate to lecturers with work experiences. As with all the other chapters, this chapter uses empirical data to support its findings. This approach is significant as it brings academic credibility to any delineations of research in the FE sector. This empirically based approach highlights the importance of this form of publication and is in cinque with disseminations with academic colleagues from the other education sectors. The framework's educational contexts, direction, and status are further developed. It further clarifies teaching knowledge and the recontextualization processes. The chapter further develops the distinctions between vocational/occupational and academic pedagogies. To this framework, two more knowledge applications are added.

The next chapter compares the teaching knowledge of teacher educators from three teaching settings: FE colleges, universities, and private providers. This comparison will offer rare insights into this under-researched group of educationists.

The fourth chapter focuses on the professional identities of FE lecturers and teacher educators. Likewise, such a comparison is rare, and much can be learnt from this investigation. One may observe that there are commonalities between these two groups of deliverers. However, the differences accord a new understanding of reflecting on these two types of deliverers/teachers through typologies and thematic analyses.

The subsequent chapter uses the systematic review of literature, which is a desktop research method and is seldom used by researchers in the FE sector. The apparent strength of this research method is that it offers the readers a comprehensive perspective of the academic publications in the chosen areas of study. Chapter 5 focuses on teacher educators' knowledge. Publications from other education sectors are also included in this research method. The chapter's research questions center on one of the sector's significant dimensions, i.e., occupational offers and commonalities and dissimilarities of each education group between the education sectors. The uniqueness of these investigations offers much needed empirical details for interested stakeholders such as researchers, master and postgraduate research students, academics, engaged FE lecturers, policymakers, and relevant networks.

The concluding chapter—Epilogue—brings together the findings of the four chapters and discusses the relevance of these findings to the FE sector. This collection of empirically supported standalone chapters adds to the relatively under-researched FE sector despite its porosity, inclusiveness, diversity, and work-weighted programmes.

References

Association of Colleges (2019) College Key Facts 2018/19. AoC, London

Education and Training Foundation (no date) So what is the FE sector? A guide to the further education system in England. ETF, London. Accessed @ 17 May 2022. https://www.et-foundation.co.uk/resources/publications/

FE News (2022) Reclassification of further education corporations, sixth form colleges into public sector, announces ONS. Accessed @ 10 Feb 2023. https://www.fenews.co.uk/fe-voices/reclassification-of-further-education-corporations-sixth-form-college-corporations-and-designated-institutions-in-england/

Frontier Economics (2020) Further education workforce data for England: analysis of the 2018–19 staff individualised (SIR) data. Education & Training Foundation, London

Loo S (2018) Teachers and teaching in vocational and professional education. Routledge, Abingdon

Loo S (2019) Further education, professional and occupational pedagogy: knowledge and experiences. Routledge, Abingdon

Loo S (2020) Professional development of teacher educators in further education: pathways, knowledge, identities, and vocationalism. Routledge, Abingdon

Loo S, Jameson J (2017) Introduction: vocationalism in the English context. In: Loo S, Jameson J (eds) Vocationalism in further and higher education: policy, programmes and pedagogy. Routledge, Abingdon

Loo S, Sutton B (2021) Informal learning, practitioner inquiry and occupational education: an epistemological perspective. Routledge, Abingdon

Chapter 2
An Epistemological Approach of Occupational/Vocational and Academic Subject Pedagogies from Teaching Perspective: Coda to the Conceptual Framework of the Occupational Pedagogy of Teachers: Mark II

Abstract Work-related pedagogy is an under-researched area in education. This chapter uses the unique conceptual framework of teachers' occupational/vocationally oriented pedagogy (Mark I) (Loo in Teachers and teaching in vocational and professional education. Routledge, Abingdon, 2018). The framework uses an English further education (FE) perspective/model as a starting basis and argues for a more inclusive and less socio-cultural-centric term of vocationally oriented education to encompass work-related nomenclature. The chapter has three aims with the related discussion sections: (a) Clarify the complex framework's contexts, direction, dynamic status, definitions of teaching know-how and recontextualization processes. (b) Delineate and develop the distinctions of vocational/occupational and academic pedagogies. (c) Include two knowledge applications of 'signature pedagogies' and 'logic of practice.' This chapter has the following sections: an introduction to set out the purpose of this submission, a discussion of the theoretical framework, details of the related project, a delineation of the empirical data with the framework and a conclusion. The conclusion section sets out the contributions of this 'Mark II' theoretical framework. They are: (a) The intellectual and practical spaces to understand and implement vocationally oriented and academic subject pedagogies. (b) Intricacies of occupational teaching and learning. (c) A comprehensive and distinct approach to knowledge acquisition, curriculum development, and teaching strategies. The implications of this chapter cover stakeholders, teacher education, teaching institutions and policy makers. Teacher educators and trainee teachers, as users, may understand, appreciate and take pride in their educational activities that are complex and dual professionally related. These stakeholders may use this framework for their professional development. Teaching institutions may support their teacher educators in their continuous professional development, and policymakers may re-think teacher training and curricula for teacher education institutions such as universities, further education colleges and private providers in England.

Keywords Occupational/vocationally oriented pedagogy · Academic subject pedagogy · Teachers' knowledge · Recontextualization · Curriculum development · Teaching strategies

Introduction

It is rare to have a theoretical framework on work-related pedagogy posited from a teacher's perspective where the teacher/lecturer also has occupational/professional experiences. This dual professionalism (Peel 2005) is a helpful starting point for thinking about vocational pedagogy. Peel (2005, p. 124) defines this concept as "dual requirements of an explicit knowledge base in their subject discipline and in ways of delivering education". This statement uses an epistemological approach (of knowledge) in both discipline (e.g., Mathematics) and education. This dual professionalism offers this chapter an epistemological perspective starting with knowledge from the discipline and education. The following section uses this approach to define the forms of knowledge and apply/implement the know-how in teaching sessions culminating in a theoretical framework. Needless to stress that these teachers deliver work-related programmes. Examples of these programmes cover areas of health and social care, heating engineering, travel and tourism at the pre-university level [equivalent to Level 4 of the European Qualifications Framework (EQF)]. These work-related programmes are known as vocational education and training (VET), offered in England or globally as technical vocational education and training (TVET) courses.[1] These work-related programmes in England include the technical qualifications (T levels) from 2020 and the new apprenticeship standards (Trailblazers).[2] Also, in England, there are higher vocational qualifications (at Level 5 and above of the EQF), including courses relating to accountancy and dental hygiene. Further up the EQF academic levels, we have professional qualifications such as clinical practices like general practitioners and emergency medicine training. This brings us to the next section on the further education (FE) sector and the English context.

The FE sector in England occupies a porous ecology. The sector is situated between the two compulsory education sectors of primary and secondary on one side and the higher education sector and professional education on the other. It is porous because its pedagogic activities overlap those of the different sectors on either side of FE. This in-betweenness is exemplified by the similarities in teaching, such as work-related courses in the secondary, higher and professional sectors. FE

---

[1] TVET was adopted by the United Nations Educational, Scientific and Cultural Organization (UNESCO) in (2012). www.unesco.org/new/en/education/themes/education-building-blocks/technical-vocational-education-and-training-tvet/third-international-congress-on-tvet/). Accessed @ 30 April 2017.

[2] https://www.cedefop.europa.eu/en/tools/vet-in-europe/systems/united-kingdom. Accessed @ 1 April 2021.

institutions also offer university-level programmes in partnership with affiliated HE institutions as accreditation bodies. These university-level courses may be at Level 5 and above the EQF. FE, historically, acts as an inclusive and widening participatory role to further former compulsory learners' lifelong learning aims. These aims include both academic and vocational studies. The diversity of its institutions complements the porosity and inclusivity of FE. "FE providers include any institutions or organisations (other than schools or universities) that receive government funding to provide education and training to people over the age of 16 (some also offer courses for 14 and 15-year-olds). There are six types of FE providers: colleges, Independent Training Providers (ITPs), Local Authority (LA) providers, employer providers, third sector providers, and Adult Community Education (ACE) providers" (Education Training Foundation no date). The largest provider is the General Further Education (GFE) Colleges with 169 colleges (67%), and the next biggest provider, 61 Sixth Form colleges (23%) out of 266 colleges in England. Vocational qualification includes Higher National Certificates/Diplomas, Technical Certificates, Technical Levels, Applied Generals, Branded Vocational Qualifications [e.g., Business and Technology Education Council (BTECs)], T Levels, Foundation Degrees, and Postgraduate Certification of Education (PGCE). Academic qualifications include General Certification of Secondary Education (GCSEs), A, AS Levels and International Baccalaureate (IB) Diplomas (ETF no date). The vocational education element accounted for 73.2% based on the number of staff by subject taught (teaching staff only), with the largest five areas: health, public services and care (11.2%) arts, media and publishing (10.7%), preparation for life and work (9.7%), engineering and manufacturing technologies (8.9%) and construction, planning and the built environment making 48.0% of the total offers in the sector (Frontier Economics 2020, Fig. 54). This diversity included 2.2 million learners in 2019, of which 1.4 million were adults, 685,000 were 16- to 18-year-olds, and 76,000 were 16- to 18-year-olds who undertook apprenticeships (Association of Colleges 2019). This vocational nature of the sector is further highlighted by the fact that 71.3% of its teaching staff teach in occupational/vocational programmes in 2017–2018 (Frontier Economics 2019), and increased to 73.2% in 2018–2019 (Frontier Economics 2020). These courses in FE are known as vocational education and training.

The above evidence highlights the porosity, inclusivity and diversity of this sector. Because of these characteristics, the FE sector is the least understood of the education sectors. Additionally, it does not have a single coherent voice. Lastly, the other significant socio-cultural factor relates to the preponderance of work-related programme offers, which are considered second to the academic ones. This 'English context' needs to be considered when investigating the FE sector (Loo and Jameson 2017).

Nearly two decades ago, Foster (2006) observed that the FE sector was like a miscreant, poorer 'middle child' of the educational landscape in England. FE appeared to be neglected amongst the compulsory and higher education sectors. Coffield (2006) was even more critical:

> England does not have an educational system, but instead three badly co-ordinated sectors - Schools, Post Compulsory and HE - which reflect sharp divisions within the Department of Education and Skills (DfES). The mental image suggested by these structural arrangements is

of three well-intentioned but dyspraxic and myopic elephants, constantly bumping into each other and standing on each other's feet instead of inter-weaving smoothly in one elegance dance.

To look further into the English FE sector and specifically at the VET system, Keep (2006) observed the strongly interventionist approach by the government to VET despite the continuous rhetorical insistence on the need for a reduction of the state, the relevance of the market and the need for institutional and individual levels of 'demand-led' ownership. For Keep (2006), the voluntarist aspect of employer engagement underpinned a continuing failure to let other stakeholders besides the government improve the VET system. This 'English model' of VET focused on specific practical individual learning outcomes for employability and work-related skills rather than on a broader knowledge-based curriculum (Brockmann et al. 2008; Clarke and Winch 2015). Thus, the focus was on skills acquisition rather than a holistic combination of theoretical knowledge, abilities and skillsets for occupational practices. Brockmann et al. (2008) contrasted the English VET approach of a skills-based model to Germany's and the Netherland's knowledge-based VET model. This narrow skills-based VET model was contrasted with the excellent higher education system and its contributions to professional expertise in England (Elsevier 2013; Blackmore 2016).

Interestingly, the research-intensive universities would not equate their professional programmes (e.g., engineering) to the VET system at pre-university levels. However, the high-performing universities with academic, professional and research activities in the UK contrasted with the under-performing VET system at the pre-university levels. There appeared to be a disconnection between vocational-related offers across the academic/qualifications framework from Levels 1–8 (EQF). Jameson and Loo (2017) argued that in the 'English model', there was a significant social class and socio-economic status schism. The schism was "between (1) the achievement of higher levels of theoretical knowledge, academic and industrial research credentials and occupational status on the one hand, in HE and the professions and (2) on the other, the gaining of lower-level employability for particular jobs through the acquisition of specific skills and training in workplace learning in FE" (Jameson and Loo 2017, p. 136).

For Jameson and Loo (2017), this disconnection between HE and FE included policy funding, local leadership and management, pedagogic quality and delivery of provision in England regarding vocational.

Wolf (2015, p. 2) re-visited Coffield's (2006) lament of the educational landscape in England:

> In England, regrettably, the 19+ education system is rarely discussed as an entity, or an interlocking system, even in the context of labour market demands for skills. Debates over higher education take place as though FE and adult training did not exist.

Wolf ended up calling for a unified approach. This chapter further develops this unified approach by its advocacy of occupational education, later in this section.

Introduction   11

The previous sections discussed the 'English context' of the FE sector with the characteristics and prominent vocationally oriented programmes, including the vocational-academic division. How does the English FE sector relate to similar sectors internationally?

Internationally, the United Nations Educational, Scientific and Culture Organization (UNESCO) (2012) used the term Technical and Vocational Education and Training (TVET) to denote the work-related provisions. However, the TVET may cover vocational programmes in higher education. My previous edited monographs included chapters on vocational contributions covering Australia, Austria, Denmark, England, Greece, India, New Zealand, Scotland and South Africa (Loo and Jameson 2017; Loo 2019, 2022). Each country has its nuanced inflexions of the vocationally oriented education landscape. Perhaps the nearest country to UNESCO's use of TVET was South Africa. Below are some examples in addition to the English system. Austria has a 'modernised traditionalism' vocational system regarding apprenticeships: training and performance occupations (Lassnigg 2019). The Australia VET system has been competency-based since the mid-1980s, with the Technical and Further Education (TAFE) as the public provider and other private providers. Denmark's vocational system aligns with lifelong learning with close dialogue with stakeholders to reflect labour market demands. The Indian government distinguishes between vocational education and vocational training. In New Zealand, vocational education is offered in the tertiary sector by institutions such as private training establishments, institutes of technologies and polytechnics, wananga, universities and workplace training. The South African government uses public TVET colleges to deliver their vocational programmes.

The previous section discussed the international context of vocationally oriented education. As mentioned earlier, there is a disconnection in the English context across the eight levels of the EQF with micro types of vocational education: VET in the pre-university sector, higher vocational in the university sector and professional education in the professions.

This chapter provides a connected nomenclature for vocationally oriented education: Occupational Education (OE).

Occupation is chosen as a vocabulary rather than vocational due to the English baggage described earlier. 'Profession' is also discounted as it has a historical-sociocultural connotation in England. It holds a more elevated position than VET and higher vocational education. Herbert Spencer observed the rise of the professions (e.g., law, medicine and science) in Victorian England. For Spencer, professions "are not only the bearers of scientific knowledge; they are also, in effect, the secular guardians of the sacred, the priesthood of the modern world, but a priesthood that acknowledges the ultimate unknowability of things, deals in uncertainties, and recognises the openness of the world to change" (Dingwall and King 1995, p. 18–19). Despite this phenomenon, Spencer was conscious of the fallibility of identifying and classifying specific professions. Instead, he offered a biological metaphor, 'occupational ecology', to delineate the permeability of these professions' boundaries. To this extent, I use OE as a continuation of Spencer's acknowledgement of the porosity of professions.

OE draws from occupational teaching, occupational learning and occupational practice. Occupational teaching may be defined as "teaching work-related courses where there is a duality of pedagogic and occupational/work-related practices and experiences, and academic teaching" (Loo 2018, p. 4). Academic teaching is related to disciplinary/theoretical knowledge and not necessarily to occupational pathways. Both work-related and academic teaching co-exists (Loo 2018). Closely associated with occupational teaching is occupational learning. This form of learning involves stakeholders, particularly learners, institutions, curriculum developers and teachers in this educational activity. The occupational practice covers the various practices that comprise occupations. These practices include "activities, models, norms, language, discourse, ways of knowing and thinking, technical capacities, knowledge, identities, philosophies and other sociocultural practices that collectively comprise their particular occupation" (Higgs 2012, p. 3). Thus, OE encompasses teaching, learning and working practices across the three EQF levels 1–8 of VET/TVET, higher and professional education. OE includes continuous professional development and training as it is work-related. So, the two aspects of occupational practice and educational activities are part of OE. OE is part of the lifelong learning spectrum of learning, working and teaching, as one expects those in such practices to be involved in ongoing professional development. OE inevitably affects education sectors and public and private industries. OE activities may cover other countries (international) and not just be confined to one education sector, such as the FE sector in England.

OE aims to seek commonalities and to reach out to the research and practitioner communities to collaborate, engage and critically research the tripartite aspects of learning, working and teaching to offer related stakeholders relevant and evidence-based findings. That is "implementable across the micro (individual-centred), meso (institutional-centred) and macro (regional, national and international-centred) levels of the discipline" (Loo 2019, p. 3–4).

The rationale for adopting OE as terminology to investigate vocationally related education are:

1. Covers all the qualification levels (1–8)
2. Incorporates the three existing work-related typologies of VET/TVET, higher vocational and professional education
3. Propounds a more neutral term compared to VET and profession
4. Offers a connected terminology, like the dual system of VET in Germany, for those in other countries to understand the English education system
5. Easily understood as 'occupation' is work-related (literally similar) but without the historical-socio-cultural baggage
6. Advances distinct pedagogical, theoretical frameworks using an epistemological approach from Bernsteinian roots (to offer academic credibility) as in this chapter
7. Provides a clear difference between work-related and academic disciplinary qualifications as in the later discussion.

The last two points will be examined later in this chapter.

The objective of this chapter is to re-assess and develop further a work-related pedagogic conceptual framework (Loo 2018).[3] Thus, the intentions of the chapter are to (1) Clarify some misunderstandings regarding the socio-cultural related contexts, non-linearity and non-static characteristics of the framework, definition of teacher's knowledge which departs from Bernstein's vertical discourse/knowledge and recontextualization process, its complexity and collaborative nature, (2) Develop further the commonalities and differences of TVET and academic subject pedagogies and intellectual space for identity formation, and (3) Include the 'signature pedagogies' (Shulman 2005) and 'logic of practice' (Bourdieu 1992) in addition to the other socio-cultural applications of 'practice architecture' (Kemmis and Grootenboer 2008), 'systems 1 and 2' (Kahneman 2012) and, 'knowledgeable practice' (Evans 2016).

In a sense, this chapter serves as a coda to the pedagogic conceptual framework, since its publication. To achieve the aims, the structure of this chapter begins with an introduction of the contexts of this conceptual framework, indication of the aims of this chapter and a structure. The next section discusses the relevant literature review relating to the framework. A section on the related project and methodologies follows next where I will draw on empirical data covering all three academic/qualification levels in the discussion section and not confined to the TVET level. The fourth section discusses the three aims using the relevant empirical data, and the final section includes a conclusion.

Literature Review and the Conceptual Framework

In this section, instead of the conventional approach of carrying out a circumscribed literature review of the relevant sources leading up to the theoretical framework, the focus is on the literature sources pertinent to this framework—Mark I (Fig. 2.1). For a fuller discussion, please refer to Chaps. 2–4 of Teachers and Teaching in Vocational and Professional Education (Loo 2018).

The framework used a dual professionalism concept (Handal 1999; Robson et al. 2004; Peel 2005), creating two dimensions: teaching practice and occupational practice. Additionally, using an epistemological approach (Burrell and Morgan 1979; Wellington 2015). Epistemology relates to the study of human knowledge regarding its nature and validity, especially the difference between knowledge and belief. The term also refers to the nature, forms, acquisition and manner of communication of

---

[3] This chapter was prompted by the panel members' responses to my keynote speech given at the Australian Vocational Education and Training Research Association (AVETRA) 2021. My special thanks to the panel members: Dr. Keiko Yasukawa, Dr. Selena Chan, Dr. John Pardy and Dr. Melina Waters for their insightful and thought-provoking comments.

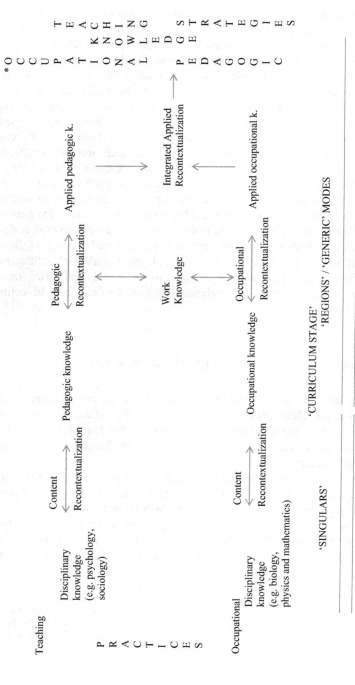

Fig. 2.1 A conceptual framework of the occupational pedagogy of teachers (mark I)

* Occupational Pedagogic Knowledge (OPK) may also be termed Occupational Teachers' Capacities (OTC)

knowledge between people. This framework concerns broader definitions of knowledge (know-how), both tacit and explicit forms, and how these may be acquired and implemented. The know-how agencies occur within the spectrum of determinism and voluntarism, which relates to stakeholders (e.g., teachers and practitioners), genetic inheritance and socio-cultural and economic environments they find themselves.

From a pedagogic delineation of knowledge, teaching may include knowledge of the relevant disciplines (Becher 1994; Bernstein 1996; Smeby 1996), such as psychology and sociology for the education field. This type of knowledge may be explicit or codified in nature (Shulman 1987; Nonaka and Takeuchi 1995; Bernstein 1996; Polanyi 1966; Verloop et al. 2001; Loughran et al. 2003; Collins 2010). Included in the relevant disciplines may be theories of learning, which teachers require to understand how learning may take place and that the related pedagogic strategies/approaches may result from the choice of the learning theory (Becher 1994; Bernstein 1996; Smeby 1996). This theoretical knowledge may be hierarchical (e.g., physics), or it may have its specialised language (e.g., social sciences) or have its mode of transmission (e.g., crafts). The latter form, known as horizontal knowledge structures, has concepts and procedures which are formally articulated (e.g., economics) or that the concepts and procedures may be informally articulated (e.g., social anthropology) (Bernstein 1996). These forms of knowledge may occur in explicit or tacit formats. Teaching knowledge may also include other forms of explicit knowledge. These are general pedagogical knowledge (consisting of principles and teaching strategies for classroom management and organisation) and pedagogical content knowledge (a combination of content and pedagogy). Also, there is knowledge of the learners, the educational contexts (e.g., of the team members and teaching institutions) and educational values (Shulman 1987). Other forms of teaching knowledge may be tacit, which require a language of articulation (Loughran et al. 2003) regarding the information, concepts and perceptions that inform teachers' practices. These pedagogic activities and the various forms of knowledge may exist individually or in collaborative formats (Loughran et al. 2003). Besides explicit and tacit teaching knowledge, there is also the cognitive variety where teachers intellectually interact with their professional learning and development and with stakeholders such as their learners and colleagues (Verloop et al. 2001; Loughran et al. 2003). Teaching knowledge may include a teacher's broader life experiences (Clandinin 1985) and occupational practices (Loo 2012). These forms of professional know-how are dynamic and process-driven, where a teacher may acquire, develop and apply her/his knowledge base over time in varying pedagogic contexts (Banks et al. 1999). The relationships between the teacher and her/his knowledge base are changed, resulting from interactions with the teacher and the external contexts such as colleagues, learners and the changing educational policies (Loo 2012). Banks et al. (1999, p. 95) describe these interactions as a "complex amalgam of past knowledge, experiences of learning, a personal view of what constitutes 'good teaching and belief'" over a period. It ought to be emphasised that a teacher's belief system may be closely associated with her/his approach to pedagogic practices.

Knowledge concerning occupational practices also requires a base of disciplinary or theoretical know-how that may be explicit. However, the theoretical knowledge used for occupational practices requires a process of application to specific work contexts and the environment in which it operates (Bernstein 1996; Loo 2012). This occupational knowledge base also includes knowledge of procedures, skills (e.g., interpersonal and intrapersonal ones which are usually tacit), techniques, transversal abilities, project management abilities, personal capabilities and occupational capacity/awareness (Eraut 2004; Winch 2014). In short, an occupational knowledge base consists of a broader spectrum than a pedagogic knowledge base. It includes a worker's prior and past know-how (including theoretical and procedural knowledge and experiences), understanding (of work and specific project contexts), skills (technical and non-technical), her/his dispositions, and the perceptions of the work environment she/he operates in. The occupational know-how involves codified and tacit types.

The other two forms of knowledge—pedagogic and occupational—may be applied through the recontextualization processes (Bernstein 1996; van Oers 1998; Barnett 2006; Evans et al. 2010; Loo 2012, 2014). They can be changed through selecting, relocating and refocusing aspects of the chosen knowledge to be used in another setting. For example, singular knowledge (e.g., psychology and biology) is used in another setting. From the teaching perspective, a learning theory such as cognitive constructivism advocated by Bruner from the discipline of psychology is used in an educational setting. This setting includes (1) contexts relating to the academic level of the programme, (2) the types of learners and (3) the specific part of the curriculum to which this knowledge is applied. From the occupational perspective, biology as knowledge from natural science may be applied in the dental hygiene occupational setting. Teachers on such a programme will use related aspects of the disciplinary knowledge (from the singulars) to deliver a session on the workings of the kidneys to dental health. From the perspective of the recontextualization process, the nature of the disciplinary knowledge is changed and similarly perceived by the users (e.g., teachers and learners) in that particular occupational area (Loo 2012, 2014) [contrary to Bernstein (1996)]. The area may include regions or generic modes such as education and dental hygiene). From a teaching perspective, the know-how can be embedded in the teaching without the learners explicitly knowing the specific part of the specifications the content is drawn from (i.e., invisible pedagogy), or the content is made known to the learners by the teachers (i.e., visible pedagogy) (Bernstein 1996).

The recontextualization process is posited in dynamic environments, involving people in socio-cultural dimensions and is context related and can be creative (van Oers 1998). It occurs in pedagogic and occupational activities that are related to work-related programmes from technical and vocational education and training (TVET), university and professional levels (Loo 2016). This process of selecting, relocating and refocusing knowledge occurs in both teaching and work-related activities. The varieties of occupational know-how consist of explicit (e.g., disciplinary knowledge and organisational procedures) and tacit (e.g., interpretation of a work activity) forms. They also cover experiences (e.g., past work-related ones), skills (e.g., detecting and

Literature Review and the Conceptual Framework

removing tooth deposits in dental hygiene), abilities (e.g., problem-solving) and dispositions (e.g., patience) (Eraut 2004; Winch 2014). The explicit/codified and tacit types of know-how may change from one type to another through collaborative working (Nonaka and Takeuchi 1995). There are also different forms of recontextualization processes. These include content recontextualization (relating to the specifications of a programme), pedagogic recontextualization (relating to teaching), learner recontextualization (relating to the strategies that are employed by the learner to acquire and understand the required knowledge), and workplace recontextualization (relating to work settings) (Evans 2016; Evans et al. 2010). The acquisition and application of occupational knowledge do not occur in a linear fashion and that there are different pathways (Loo 2012, 2014). Thus, a teacher of dental hygiene may teach on the programme at the same time as practising in that occupational area. She/he may not necessarily have a teaching qualification at the start of the teaching career, but this may be acquired at a later date. The nature of her/his knowledge/know-how is changed from the person's perspective through specific and contextual applications of that know-how especially in relation to the occupational relevance.

Related concepts offer additional insights into how a teacher with pedagogic and occupational experiences can apply her/his know-how. These concepts include knowledgeable practice (Evans 2016), developed through formal and informal learning in the workplace and outside. They also cover practice architecture (Kemmis and Green 2013), which is carried out in organizations, institutions and settings where a teacher can use her/his 'sayings', 'doings', and 'relatings'. Furthermore, Systems 1 and 2 (Kahneman 2012), where the former is intuitively based on past experiences and the latter relies on rational and cognitive interactions.

In this framework, both teaching and occupational practices are related to knowledge: acquisition and application. This structuring approach was intended as a discussion device as the commonalities and entanglements of the two practices might not be disassociated in real life. I will use the two dimensions as sections in the discussion below.

Teaching Practice

This dimension of the framework (upper part of Fig. 2.1) relates to an occupational teacher's epistemological agencies: meaning that s/he needs to acquire and utilize/implement knowledge in her/his teaching activities. Reading Fig. 2.1 from left to right, thus, a health and social care teacher in an FE college (VET), a dental hygiene lecturer at a university (higher vocational) or a lecturer training doctors (professional education) will refer initially to the teaching knowledge. This knowledge type may be derived from psychology, sociology and business management. Examples may be learning theories such as social constructivism and behaviourism.[4] This knowledge/know-how relating to the 'singulars' needs to be recontextualized (Bernstein 1996; van Oers 1998; Barnett 2006; Evans et al. 2010; Loo 2012, 2014, 2018). So that it can be used as theoretical knowledge for teaching purposes, meaning that the chosen disciplinary learning theories are theoretical knowledge, to begin with. For teaching purposes, this knowledge needs to be recontextualized to the relevant teaching programme, such as the health and social care course (VET), dental hygiene (higher vocational) or training of doctors (professional education) and the specific aspects of the relevant curriculum/specification. This type of recontextualization process is called content recontextualization (Evans et al. 2010; Loo 2018). After this process, the knowledge becomes pedagogic knowledge. From a Bernsteinian (1996) perspective, the forms of theoretical knowledge might be dependent on the two types of vertical pedagogic knowledge: hierarchical (e.g., psychology) or horizontal knowledge structures (e.g., sociology). Since the pedagogic knowledge is used further in classroom contexts, another recontextualization process is required.

This second process is known as pedagogic recontextualization (Evans et al. 2010). In this process, the pedagogic knowledge is selected and refocused for use in teaching sessions. This stage of the teaching dimension becomes part of the application of pedagogic knowledge. It includes two types of knowledge: pedagogic knowledge (as described above) and work knowledge. The latter typically refers to work experiences of a pedagogic nature. This know-how relates to experiences in teaching organizations such as an FE college or a university. These experiences cover systems and protocols of working in the teaching institutions and experiences of being mentored, coached or via peer learning. These experiences may be individual or collective. The know-how may be explicit or tacit, involving skillsets (e.g., interpersonal, thinking and learning), knowledge resources (from the Internet and colleagues), understanding (of situations, contexts and stakeholders) and decision-making and judgement (Evans et al. 2010; Loo 2018). Concepts such as 'knowledgeable practice' (Evans 2016), 'practice architecture' (Kemmis and Green 2013) and 'Systems 1 and 2 (Kahneman 2012) are useful in understanding this application process. This first approach concerns formal and informal learning in the workplace and outside (Evans 2016). The second approach covers a teacher's 'sayings', 'doings' and 'relatings' in teaching settings (Kemmis and Green 2013). The third approach refers to decision-making based on intuition based on past experiences (System 1) and rational and cognitive interactions (System 2) (Kahneman 2012).

The two knowledge types: pedagogic and work, are used in the second pedagogic recontextualization process. The resulting knowledge is called applied pedagogic knowledge. This know-how undergoes a final recontextualization process with the know-how from the occupational practice dimension before the final knowledge can be applied in the classroom. The end of this teaching practice dimension leads us onto the next dimension involving knowledge in occupational practice.

---

[4] Please refer to 'Theories of Learning' on the website: https://ioe.academia.edu SaiLoo for a visual representation of the major learning theories and their relationships.

Occupational Practice

This lower dimension (Fig. 2.1) refers to an occupational worker's working and learning processes. From a work perspective, this relates to an occupational teacher of a VET, higher vocational or a professional education programme working in his/her occupational practice. This worker will follow similar recontextualization processes to the earlier teaching practice dimension.

A worker (and eventual teacher) acquires the relevant disciplinary knowledge (such as physics, mathematics or biology) for use in the relevant occupation (e.g., gas fitting, accountancy or emergency medicine). Again, like in the teaching practice dimension, this disciplinary knowledge is selected, modified and relocated for the appropriate occupation. This is the content recontextualization process, and after this process, the modified knowledge is called occupational knowledge. For example, the pertinent aspects of physics, such as gas flow knowledge, will be used for the worker or learner for gas fitting work. This know-how is different to the disciplinary knowledge form as it is contextualized to the specific occupational needs. From a learner's perspective, this disciplinary knowledge is contextualized to his/her specific occupation and is, therefore, different to someone who knows this know-how purely from a disciplinary perspective.

This know-how is used to frame a curriculum as part of its specifications. Like in the other dimension, this is the conceptual framework's acquisition phase using a singular form of vertical discourse (Bernstein 1996). The occupational knowledge undergoes another recontextualization process known as occupational recontextualization. This second recontextualization process involves two types of know-how. The first is occupational knowledge, modified from recontextualized disciplinary knowledge such as physics in gas fitting and anatomy and psychology in dental hygiene. The second knowledge type is work knowledge. This knowledge involves the know-how of organizational systems, protocols and other aspects other than occupational know-how. It has individual and collective dimensions. These forms of know-how can be explicit or tacit. They can consist of skillsets (e.g., interpersonal, thinking and learning), knowledge resources (from the Internet and colleagues), understanding (of situations, contexts and stakeholders) and decision-making and judgement. One may suggest that the occupational and work knowledge is specific to him/her. The specific occupational and work experiences (e.g., initial clinical training and experiences of patients are specific to the doctor) are different to those in the same occupational area (e.g., emergency medicine). The earlier application approaches, such as 'knowledgeable practice' (Evans 2016), 'practice architecture' (Kemmis and Green 2013), and 'Systems 1 and 2' (Kahneman 2012). These approaches provide a richer understanding of the complex activity regarding the institutional protocols, the 'sayings', 'doings' and 'relatings' of the workers and the decision-making processes in carrying out the occupational activities.

The complex amalgam of occupational and work knowledge of an occupational nature via the occupational recontextualization process becomes applied occupational knowledge. The applied occupational knowledge from the occupational practice dimension and the applied pedagogic knowledge from the teaching practice dimension undergo a final recontextualization process: the integrated applied recontextualization (IAR) process. The result of the final process is known as occupational pedagogic knowledge. A teacher with occupational experience teaching on a work-related programme may not consciously relate to the above types of know-how and processes. This IAR process results in the final form of occupational pedagogic knowledge (OPK). OPK is the relocated and refocused knowledge from the pedagogic and occupational forms of know-how. OPK allows the teacher with occupational know-how to choose the best possible teaching strategies for teaching to a specific cohort of learners on a particular work-related programme at a specific academic level and a specific aspect of the curriculum.

This complex amalgam of teaching and occupational know-how provides a deeper understanding of the convoluted processes of delivering a work-related programme. In the discussion section, I will clarify relevant aspects of the Mark I framework, further develop the framework to delineate the vocational and academic subject pedagogies offering intellectual space for identity formation and include two supporting applications in the implementation stage. Application of the conceptual framework requires acknowledgement and understanding of the relevant contexts.

Research Project

The empirical data in this chapter is based on a project with two leading research aims. The first was related to defining vocationally oriented education across the education landscape in England. The second aim asked how the related knowledge might be acquired and applied by those teaching in the relevant programmes. The project used a mixed-research method of survey and semi-structured one-to-one interviews together with the inevitable literature review of related documents (e.g., course specifications and government reports) and sources. Salient quantitative data such as gender, age group, academic qualifications, teaching experiences and occupational/professional experiences were captured using a questionnaire. From the interviews, rich and textured data was obtained relating to the participants' perspectives in teaching, relevant pedagogic know-how and application. In this purposive data capture of teachers/lecturers in England (Robson and McCartan 2016), connected networks (e.g., the British Educational Research Association (BERA), Learning and Skills Research Network and Teacher Educator UK) of the further, higher and professional education sectors were approached. Twenty-one occupational participants (OPs) took part in this project, with seven from each of the three education sectors. Teachers of the related work-related programmes such as equine studies and leisure and tourism (from FE), dental hygiene and accountancy (HE), and training of general practitioners and emergency medicine (professional education) took part in the project. A pilot study was carried out following the ethical approval of the Principal Investigator's institution. The standard procedures of data captured starting with an initial approach by an introductory email and followed up with Information Sheet and Consent Form. Willing participants were issued with the survey to complete and followed by an interview. The captured quantitative and qualitative data were analysed and triangulated with supporting documents and sources (Williams and Vogt 2014; Cohen et al. 2018). The stages of the project adhered to the BERA Ethical Guidelines (2018) together with the institution's ethical regulations concerning anonymity, storage, security and other related issues.

Discussion

This section focuses on the three themes indicated at the introduction of this chapter relating to clarifying misunderstandings of theoretical framework, developing further TVET and academic subject pedagogies, and including 'signature pedagogies' and 'logic of practice' implementation processes.

Clarification of Misunderstandings

This theme covers misunderstandings concerning the framework's contexts/dimensions, its direction of travel and dynamism, definitions of teaching know-how and recontextualization processes departing from Bernstein's (1996) related concepts, and the framework's complexity and collaborative nature.

The conceptual framework (Fig. 2.1) subscribes to a multi-dimensional/contextual approach to sociology, culture, economics, and politics. The framework uses researchers such as Bernstein (1996) and Evans (2016), who offer a socio-cultural context. Others, such as Kemmis and Grootenboer (2008, p. 57), construct their 'practice architecture' concept in "cultural-discursive, social-political and material-economic dimensions". These multi-dimensions provide a micro perspective of occupational teachers with educational and work practice experiences. Supporting the micro views of these teachers are the broader dimensions of socio-cultural (e.g., learners' needs within a more comprehensive societal environment and academic-vocational division in England), economics (e.g., funding of the programmes), and politics (e.g., education policies). So, it is helpful to remember that the educational and occupational practices are related to socio-cultural, economic and political dimensions, so the discussions are refracted to the relevant dimensions. These dimensions are related to the next theme on the direction of travel and dynamics of this framework.

An example of this is OP5. She practised as a fashion designer and taught in an art and design programme at an FE college. Her knowledge (for teaching and occupational practices) comes from various sources such as operas, plays, ballet, myths, fairy tales, religions and culture. She used inspirations from the McQueen exhibition (fashion and culture) from the Victoria and Albert Museum, London, Gloriana (opera associated with Queen Elizabeth I) and Petrushka (ballet associated with Russia) in her teaching. She also used these iconic projects to inform her students of the economic (e.g., costing of the materials and tangentially course funding) and politics (e.g., colonial and political links of McQueen's fashion and Gloriana's opera relating to Queen Elizabeth I and the Spanish Armada in 1588).

The framework provides bi-directional arrows from left to right and does not necessarily follow a start-to-finish pathway. For example, OP9, a dental hygienist who practised as one in a dental practice and taught in the first-degree programme in dental hygiene at a university, enrolled on a university-based teacher education programme after having taught in the dental hygiene programme for several years before that. She had 14 years of teaching experience and 31 years as a dental hygienist at the start of the project. She would have covered the two recontextualization processes via the occupational practice dimension from the framework perspective. However, at the teaching practice pathway, she had past teaching experiences. Thus, her teaching experiences enabled her to go through the pedagogic recontextualization process. But not the content recontextualization stage (i.e., she did not formally cover the learning theories). These would have been delivered whilst on the teacher education programme.

Similarly, an occupational lecturer might have reflected after a teaching session and had to refer back to a learning theory or disciplinary/theoretical knowledge to re-access future teaching approaches. Another possibility is the teacher might want to re-think the past occupational experiences in her occupational practice (e.g., dental hygiene). This reflective loop of going back to the theoretical base is possible. This framework is also dynamic and is not constrained by time. The framework offers an occupational lecturer to reflect and return to theories (pedagogic or occupational) or past experiences (academic and occupational) to facilitate her teaching for a specific session. Contexts govern the session, whether educational, occupational, socio-cultural, economic or political.

The definition of teaching know-how is broad, covering disciplinary/theoretical knowledge, pedagogic and occupation-related knowledge, experiences, capacities/ abilities and skill sets. These forms of know-how may be explicit or implicit, unlike Bernstein's narrow vertical discourse. Even though the framework started from a Bernsteinian epistemological perspective, it defines teaching know-how widely (Shulman 1987; Verloop et al. 2001; Loughran et al. 2003; Eraut 2004; Loo 2012, 2014; Winch 2014). OP19, a teacher of the undergraduate medical education and a general practitioner who worked in the banking and mobile communications industries, described her broad range of know-how:

> Medicine is a difficult subject as students need to acquire much factual knowledge...they also need life skills, communication skills and learn to be leaders and managers...learn to reflect...we have home visits. They need to write about situations relating to questions such as what struck them, are there any worries and other deeply emotional issues.

Discussion 23

The recontextualization principle subscribed by Bernstein again offers a narrow perspective of the relocation and modification of his vertical knowledge. However, this framework subscribes to a broader definition of knowledge for recontextualization. Loo (2014) showed, using empirical data (unlike Bernstein's theoretical approach), that his ongoing recontextualization process is modified and relocated constantly. The process might include teaching know-how types, theoretical/disciplinary, pedagogic and occupational knowledge, experiences, abilities and skillsets. This process is to make relevant the purpose of either educational or occupational contexts.

One questions Bernstein's immutability of the vertical and horizontal discourses. Despite the modification/recontextualization of his vertical knowledge, this knowledge remains modified and explicit. As the author's empirical findings show, the recontextualized know-how is changed. This modified know-how is both explicit and implicit together with the complex combination of other forms of know-how, including experiences, intuition, beliefs, capabilities and skillsets, as shown by Nonaka and Takeuchi's (1995) empirical findings with their work on innovative business practices in large Japanese companies.

The last point refers to the framework's complexities and collaborative nature. Loo (2012) clarified five complexities of the occupational pedagogy of teachers, and this framework is posited in that arena. Verloop et al. (2001), Loughran et al. (2003), and Nonaka and Takeuchi (1995) show how collaborative working is a significant feature in their findings. This collaborative aspect of work is summed up by OP16, an Emergency Medicine consultant and teacher:

> I have changed how I talk to people, reflect and work things through with them. (e.g., the numerous stakeholders in this collaborative role in EM)

Further Development of TVET and Academic Subject Pedagogies and Intellectual Space for Identity Formation

This part highlights the differences between occupational and academic subject pedagogies from the framework's perspective (Mark II, Fig. 2.2) and includes the intellectual spaces for identity formation.

The apparent differences between occupational and academic subject pedagogies are not commonly explained. This conceptual framework offers a visual and descriptive understanding. OP14, a practising dental hygienist and lecturer of a first-degree programme of the same occupation, describes the differences between the related disciplinary and dental hygiene knowledge:

> Pure biology relates to areas such as neck/oral, health and promotion, smoking, etc. In contrast, knowledge associated with dental hygiene comes naturally as I am practising and have already acquired the knowledge – second nature. I view this as occupational relevance.

For OP14, the related disciplinary knowledge, such as anatomy, differs from the associated dental hygiene knowledge. The latter was made 'occupationally relevant'

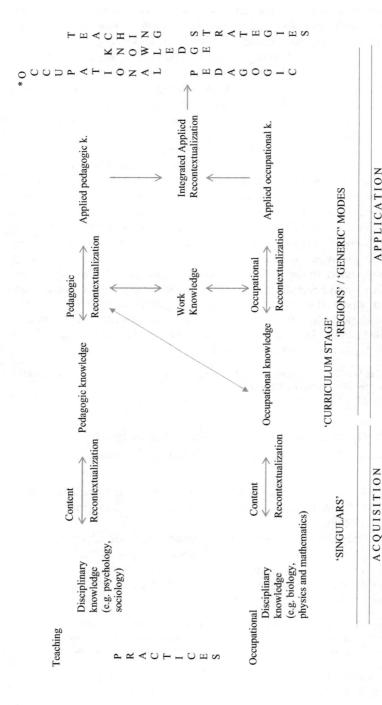

Fig. 2.2 A conceptual framework of the occupational pedagogy of teachers (mark II)

* Occupational Pedagogic Knowledge (OPK) may also be termed Occupational Teachers' Capacities (OTC)

for use in that occupational practice: forming the first part of the occupational practice dimension (Fig. 2.2). The recontextualized occupational knowledge can then be used for occupational purposes. In contrast, after the content recontextualization process (part of the curriculum development stage), a teacher of pure biology or anatomy will use aspects of the course specification to disseminate the knowledge to the students. One might call this recontextualized knowledge: recontextualized academic subject knowledge (not indicated in Fig. 2.2). The previous points illustrate the essential difference between occupational and academic subject teaching. The former applies the occupational knowledge in the relevant occupation.

In contrast, the latter is used for academic subject teaching (as shown by the arrow towards the pedagogic recontextualization process in Fig. 2.2). In the academic subject teaching practice pathway, disciplinary knowledge such as psychology (e.g., learning theories) would need to be modified via the content recontextualization process to make it relevant for the pure biology curriculum. The recontextualized knowledge is known as pedagogic knowledge (PK).

It is helpful to pause here to reflect on the related concepts regarding academic subjects. Here, we turn to Dewey (1977, p. 362–6) with his insights regarding teacher's and learner's perspectives:

> [W]hat concerns him [Dewey], as a teacher, is the ways in which that subject may become a part of experience; what there is in the child's present that is usable with reference to it; how such elements are to be used; how his own knowledge of the subject-matter may assist in interpreting the child's needs and doings and determine the medium in which the child should be placed in order that his growth may be properly directed. He is concerned, not with the subject-matter as such, but with the subject-matter as a related factor in a total and growing experience.

Shulman and Quinlan (1996) call Dewey's perspectives psychologizing the subject matter, which has two aspects. One relates to the subject matter to the discovery process: the other is a transformation of the subject matter into something meaningful and educative to the learner. From the perspectives of this chapter, Dewey, and Shulman, and Quinlan appear to be resonating with the concepts of Verloop et al. (2001) and Loughran et al. (2003), where a teacher's know-how (including theoretical and educational knowledge that is explicit and implicit) and knowledge of learners are part of the teaching dimension. These forms of educational know-how also cover knowledge, experiences and the broader socio-cultural contexts (and more) that teachers find themselves in any classroom setting. Interpreting the learners' needs and doings resonates with Kemmis and Green's (2013) practice architecture in thinking about how know-how may be applied in a classroom setting through the enactions and interactions with the stakeholders (especially learners) and the broader dimensions of social, cultural, etc. Shulman and Quinlan (1996) mention transforming the subject matter into a meaningful process for learners. The previous point has resonance with the concept of recontextualization (Bernstein 1996; Evans et al. 2010; Loo 2012, 2014). With this situation, know-how may be changed, relocated and made relevant to the specific educative practice with the ultimate purpose of a learner being able to understand and apply the newly acquired know-how in her/his educational setting. The setting might be programme related at a specific academic level or for a particular occupational practice. In short, this detour in academic subject teaching aims to show commonalities between the theoretical and pedagogical perspectives of occupational teaching practices.

Returning to PK, the recontextualized academic subject knowledge and work knowledge (i.e., teaching institution's systems and protocols) need to be relocated and modified via the pedagogic recontextualization process to become the now changed pedagogic knowledge for classroom application. Teachers of this academic subject can choose the appropriate teaching strategy or strategies to teach students a particular part of the curriculum at an academic level. The more complex occupational pedagogic process requires a further stage of recontextualization. Combining applied pedagogic and applied occupational know-how. The process is known as the integrated applied recontextualization process before choosing the relevant teaching strategy or strategies for work-related learners. OP9, the dental hygienist, sums up the complexity of occupational pedagogy:

> Challenging mix of disciplinary and pedagogic knowledge and experiences (teaching, occupational and life) to bring together in a teaching session.

Concerning identity formation, one refers to Bernstein (1996). He provided three rules of the pedagogic device to suggest that these were connected to a teacher's professional identity. These are 'distributive rules' (i.e., vertical and horizontal discourses), 'recontextualization rules' (i.e., the relocation or modification of vertical discourse/knowledge), and 'evaluative rules' (i.e., a transformation of stakeholders' pedagogic discourse via the recontextualization rules). Bernstein (1996, p. 73) suggests that "identity arises out of a particular social order through relations which the identity enters into with other identities of reciprocal collective purpose". For him, the collective process is in enacting the three pedagogic devices. Bernstein's theories offer intellectual space for teachers' identities to form from vertical knowledge via his distributive rules. In this occupational pedagogy of teachers' framework, Bernstein's ideas provide an opening to relating teachers' know-how to their professional identity formation. Perhaps, a further note with concepts by Bernstein (1996), other school-related researchers (e.g., Loughran et al. 2003) and knowledge application-related researchers (e.g., Evans 2016; Kemmis and Green 2013), one may infer that the concepts cover ideas of inclusion and social equity. In short, this conceptual framework (Fig. 2.2) subscribes to these developments.

Inclusion of Two Further Implementation Approaches: 'Signature Pedagogies' (Shulman 2005) and 'Logic of Practice' (Bourdieu 1992)

This third theme focuses on two knowledge application theories of 'signature pedagogies' (Shulman 2005) and 'logic of practice' (Bourdieu 1992).

Shulman (2005) described his 'signature of pedagogies' as having these characteristics. They are 'habitual, routine, visible, accountable, interdependent, collaborative, emotional, unpredictable, and affect-laden.[5] He further identified three pedagogies: uncertainty, engagement, and formation. With a pedagogy of uncertainty, the teacher's responses depend on the learners' reactions to one another and the teacher's adaptations. He argued that the teacher should be prepared for contingencies despite meticulous lesson planning. Shulman viewed professions as fields where people make decisions and act under conditions of unavoidable uncertainty. He saw this type of uncertainty as a way of socialising new professionals into this practice.

Regarding 'engagement', learners and deliverers need to engage to facilitate learning. With 'formation', this kind of pedagogic descriptor relates to building identity, character, dispositions and values. For Shulman, this pedagogy of formation offers 'habits of mind' and 'habits of the heart' because of the 'marriage of reason, interdependence and emotion'. In response to teacher education, his response was to veer away from the notion of 'best practice' as these best practices emerged contextually, historically, in settings.

Shulman identified the 'signature of pedagogies' from the professions of law, medicine, engineering and the clergy. His definition of a profession relates to practitioners who make decisions and perform under conditions of uncertainty. One might suggest that those in occupational practices such as health and social care, travel and tourism (TVET), and accountancy and dental hygiene (higher vocational) also make decisions and perform under uncertain conditions. As early as eighteenth century Britain, Herbert Spencer, a contemporary of Charles Darwin, realised the difficulties of defining a profession and suggested the rise of the professions of law, medicine and science was a consequence of a movement from a more superficial society to a complex or industrial society. This rise of the professions arose from two factors: (1) the ecological competition and (2) the differentiation of a society where people were required to cooperate. Spencer agreed with his French contemporary, Emile Durkheim, that religious institutions had a hand in societal evolution (Dingwall and King 1995). Shulman's choices of the professions, including the clergy, perhaps have their etymological derivations from the eighteenth century thinkers.

Regarding the conceptual framework of the occupational pedagogy of teachers, Shulman's signature pedagogies offer overlaps concerning his identified professions (the anomaly is the clergy). His signature pedagogies are posited in socio-historical contexts. This last point has resonance with the conceptual framework. Because he has not provided a conceptual framework but a listing of characteristics, his signature pedagogies are more related to an application to teaching than acquisition. This applied approach sits nicely in the application part of the conceptual framework as with the others, such as 'knowledgeable practices' (Evans 2016) and 'practice architecture' (Kemmis and Green 2013).

---

[5] The text was not paginated.

Bourdieu (1992, p. 92) views 'logic of practice' as "logic which, like all practical logics, can only be grasped in action, in the temporal moment that disguises it by detemporalizing it, sets the analyst a complex problem, which can only be solved by recourse to a theory of theoretical logic and practical logic".

Silva and Wade (2010) offered four perspectives on evaluating Bourdieu's work: defending the legacy, partial appropriation, critical revisions, and repudiation. The first perspective amounted to an acceptance of his work, the second view offered an overall agreement with caveats, and the third perspective acknowledged the virtues of Bourdieu's theory (e.g., of habitus) but had shortcomings in certain aspects (such as the concepts of field, cultural capital, and habitus). Regarding the last perspective, an argument for its abandonment.

Perhaps, from a practical implementation viewpoint, Smith and Tinning (2011, p. 245) provide the most reasoned response to using Bourdieu's concept as it offered "an inherent, underpinning, subconscious logic of practice". Regarding this chapter, teachers need to embrace a subconscious ideological belief embodied in the conceptual framework of the occupational pedagogy of teachers.

Bourdieu's practice concept is context-related and thus identified with action at a specific moment. The 'analyst' can resolve this activity through logic related to theory and practice. Accepting there is criticism as with any concept, including a lack of a theoretical structure/framework, posited in theoretical discussion without empirical data, and practical applicability of the concept. Lau (2004, p. 376) offered a way forward in his view, Bourdieu's 'practice' as "emerging from experience is consistent with the argument that habitus is objectivist". By objectivist, Lau (2004, p. 370) meant it is "not necessarily deterministic reductionist".

Relating this point to the conceptual framework, Bourdieu's 'practice of logic' provides another possible angle to understanding the application of know-how (both pedagogic and occupation-related) in teaching where the teaching practice is grounded as an activity at a specific point in time. For Bourdieu, it is a practice that provides a real understanding of social reality. The teacher, as an analyst, approaches this practice using theoretical and practical logic. The theoretical elements might have commonalities with theoretical know-how, such as disciplinary knowledge that might be less affected by human perception. The practical element might be related to agencies of doing (Kemmis and Green 2013) with Husserl's (1989) notions of 'intuitive expectations' or 'practical anticipation' (Nonaka and Takeuchi 1995).

Conclusion

This conceptual framework applies explicitly to all occupation/work-related programmes. The chapter has delineated the framework. I have defined and identified a new research area—occupational education—to encompass TVET, higher vocational and professional education across the three academic levels of pre-university, higher and professional education. This chapter provided three aims. One was clarification of socio-cultural contexts, non-linearity and dynamic characteristics of the framework, definitions of teachers' know-how and recontextualization, and the framework's complexities. The second aim centred on further developments in the framework by highlighting the differences between occupational and academic subject pedagogies and discussing the possible intellectual space regarding identity formation. The final aim focused on the inclusions of two knowledge applications of 'signature pedagogies' by Shulman and 'logic of practice' by Bourdieu. These two applications complemented the other knowledge applications of 'knowledgeable practices' (Evans 2016), 'five complexities of occupational pedagogy (Loo 2012), 'ongoing recontextualization' (Loo 2014), 'practice architecture' (Kemmis and Green 2013), and Systems 1 and 2 (Kahneman 2012).

The chapter's contributions include intellectual and practical spaces to understand and implement occupational and academic subject pedagogies. The distinction offers a rare discussion or, instead, the beginning of discourse between the artificial constructions of the pedagogies. The conceptual framework shows commonalities, and this approach may offer a richer dialogue than an opposing stance. Occupational pedagogy is complex and, judging from the suggested conceptual framework, more convoluted than academic subject pedagogy. The dual professional framework provides a throughput approach from theoretical knowledge of the disciplines to curriculum development (i.e., knowledge acquisition) and to teaching deliveries via the choices of teaching strategies (i.e., knowledge application).

The implications cover how teachers (occupational and academic subjects) are trained using an epistemological perspective. This teacher education approach facilitates collaborative interactions between teacher educators and related teacher education programmes. For example, England's compulsory secondary education and further education sectors offer work-related programmes. From the policymaking perspective, the relevant stakeholders may have a more joined-up teacher education/training and curricula policy. Delivery institutions such as universities, colleges and private providers may better support their managers, teacher educators, and trainee teachers/learners in understanding the deliveries of the curricula. Finally, the users, such as teachers and teacher educators, may understand, appreciate and take pride in their pedagogic roles, which are complex and dual professional-related. These characteristics would have implications for the educationists' continuous professional development needs.

References

Association of Colleges (2019) College key facts 2018/19. AoC, London
Banks F, Leach J, Moon B (1999) New understandings of teachers' pedagogic knowledge. In: Leach, J, Moon B (eds) Learners and pedagogy. Paul Chapman Publishing, London
Barnett M (2006) Vocational knowledge and vocational pedagogy. In: Young M, Gamble J (eds) Knowledge, curriculum and qualifications for South African further education. Human Sciences Research Council Press, Cape Town
Becher T (1994) The significance of disciplinary differences. Stud High Educ 19:151–161. https://doi.org/10.1080/03075079412331382007

Bernstein B (1996) Pedagogy, symbolic control and identity: theory, research, critique. Taylor and Francis Limited, London

Blackmore P (2016) Prestige in academic life: excellence and exclusion. Routledge, Abingdon

Bourdieu P (1992) Logic of practice. Polity Press, Bristol

British Education Research Association (BERA) (2018) Ethical guidelines for educational research. BERA, London

Brockmann M, Clarke L, Winch C (2008) Knowledge, skills, competence: European divergences in vocational education and training (VET)—the English, German and Dutch cases. Oxf Rev Educ 34(5):547–567

Burrell G, Morgan G (1979) Sociological paradigms and organizational analysis. Heinemann Educational Books, London

Clandinin J (1985) Personal practical knowledge: a study of teachers' classroom images. Curric Inq 15(4):361–385. https://doi.org/10.1080/03626784.1985.11075976

Clarke L, Winch C (2015) Have Anglo-Saxon concepts really influenced the development of European qualifications policy? Res Comp Int Educ 10:593–606

Coffield F (2006) Running ever faster down the wrong road: an alternative future for education and skills. Inaugural Lecture at the Institute of Education. Institute of Education, University of London, London, England, 5 Dec 2006

Cohen L, Manion L, Morrison K (2018) Research methods in education. Routledge, Abingdon

Collins H (2010) Tacit and explicit knowledge. University of Chicago Press, Chicago

Dewey J (1977) The child and the curriculum. In: Boydston A (ed) John Dewey. The middle works 1899–1924, vol 2. Southern Illinois University Press, Carbondale, Illinois, p 19021903

Dingwall R, King MD (1995) Herbert spencer and the professions: occupational ecology reconsidered. Sociol Theory 13(1):13–24

Education and Training Foundation (no date) So what is the FE sector? A guide to the further education system in England. ETF, London. Accessed @ 17 May 2022. https://www.et-foundation.co.uk/resources/publications/

Elsevier (2013) International comparative performance of the UK research base—2013. Report commissioned by the UK Department for Business, Innovation and Skills (BIS). BIS, London. Retrieved Feb 2016. https://www.gov.uk/government/uploads/system/uploads/attachment_data/file/263729/bis-13-1297-international-comparative-performance-of-the-UK-research-base-2013.pdf

Eraut M (2004) Transfer of knowledge between education and workplace settings. In: Rainbird H, Fuller A, Munro A (eds) Workplace learning in context. Routledge, Abingdon

Evans K (2016) Higher vocational learning and knowledgeable practice: the newly qualified practitioner at work. In: Loo S, Jameson J (eds) Vocationalism in further and higher education: policy, programmes and pedagogy. Routledge, Abingdon

Evans K, Guile D, Harris J, Allan H (2010) Putting knowledge to work: a new approach. Nurse Educ Today 30(3):245–251. https://doi.org/10.1016/j.nedt.2009.10.014

Foster A (2006) Realising the potential: a review of the future role of further education colleges (the foster report). Department of Education and Skills, London

Frontier Economics (2019) Further education workforce data for England: analysis of the 2017–18 staff individualised (SIR) data. Education & Training Foundation, London

Frontier Economics (2020) Further education workforce data for England: analysis of the 2018–19 staff individualised (SIR) data. Education & Training Foundation, London

Handal G (1999) Consultation using critical friends. New Dimens Teach Learn 79:59–70

Higgs J (2012) Practice-based education: the practice-education-context-quality nexus. In: Higgs J, Barnett R, Billett S, Hutchings M, Trede F (eds) Practice-based education: perspectives and strategies (practice, education, work and society). Sense Publishers, Rotterdam

Husserl E (1989) Ideas pertaining to a pure phenomenology and to a phenomenological philosophy, second book, studies in the phenomenology of constitution (trans. Rojecwicz R, Schuwer A). Kluwer Academic Publishers

Jameson J, Loo S (2017) Conclusion: global perspectives on vocationalism and the English model. In: Loo S, Jameson J (eds) Vocationalism in further and higher education: policy, programmes and pedagogy. Routledge, Abingdon

Kahneman D (2012) Thinking, fast and slow. Penguin Books, London

Keep E (2006) State control of the English education and training system—playing with the biggest train set in the world. J Vocat Educ Train 58(1):47–64

Kemmis RB, Green A (2013) Vocational education and training teachers' conceptions of their pedagogy. Int J Train Res 11(2):101–121. https://doi.org/10.5172/ijtr.2013.11.2.101

Kemmis S, Grootenboer P (2008) Situating praxis in practice: practice architectures and the cultural, social and material conditions for practice. In: Kemmis S, Smith TJ (eds) Enabling praxis: challenges for education. Sense, Rotterdam, The Netherlands

Lassnigg L (2019) 'Ausbildungsberufe'—a necessary and complex ingredient of the 'Dual' apprenticeship frameworks. In: Loo S (ed) Multiple dimensions of teaching and learning for occupational practice. Routledge, Abingdon

Lau RWK (2004) Habitus and the practical logic of practice: an interpretation. Sociology 38(2):369–387. https://doi.org/10.1177/0038038504040870

Loo S (2012) The application of pedagogic knowledge to teaching: a conceptual framework. Int J Lifelong Learn 31(6):705–723

Loo S (2014) Placing 'knowledge' in teacher education in the English further education teaching sector: an alternative approach based on collaborative and evidence-based research. Br J Educ Stud 62(3):337–354

Loo S (2016) Training of teachers of occupation-related programmes. In: Gibbs IS (ed) Teacher education: assessment, impact and social perspectives. Nova Science Publishers Inc., Hauppauge, NY

Loo S (2018) Teachers and teaching in vocational and professional education. Routledge, Abingdon

Loo S (ed) (2019) Multiple dimensions of teaching and learning for occupational practice. Routledge, Abingdon

Loo S (2020) Professional development of teacher educators in further education: pathways, knowledge, identities, and vocationalism. Routledge, Abingdon

Loo S (ed) (2022) Teacher educators in vocational and further education. Springer, Cham

Loo S, Jameson J 2017 (Eds.) Vocationalism in further and higher education: policy, programmes and pedagogy. Abingdon, Routledge

Loo S, Jameson J (2017) Introduction: vocationalism in the English context. In: Loo S, Jameson J (eds) Vocationalism in further and higher education: policy, programmes and pedagogy. Routledge, Abingdon

Loughran J, Mitchell I, Mitchell J (2003) Attempting to document teachers' professional knowledge. Qual Stud Educ 16(6):853–873. https://doi.org/10.1080/0951839030001632180

Nonaka I, Takeuchi H (1995) The knowledge creating company: how Japanese companies create the dynamics of innovation. Oxford University Press, Oxford

Peel D (2005) Dual professionalism: Facing the challenges of continuing professional development in the workplace? Reflect Pract Int Multidisc Perspect 6(1):123–149. https://doi.org/10.1080/1462394042000326851

Polanyi M (1966) The tacit dimension. Routledge and Kegan Paul, London

Robson C, McCartan K (2016) Real world research. UK, Wiley, Chichester

Robson J, Bailey B, Larkin S (2004) Adding value: investigating the discourse of professionalism adopted by vocational teachers in further education colleges. J Educ Work 17(2):183–195. https://doi.org/10.1080/1363908041001677392

Shulman LS (1987) Knowledge and teaching: foundations of the new reform. Harvard Educ Rev 57(1):1–22. https://doi.org/10.17763/haer.57.1.j463w79r56455411

Shulman LS (2005) The signature pedagogies of the professions of law, medicine, engineering, and the clergy: potential lessons for the education of teachers. In: The math science partnerships workshop: "teacher education for effective teaching and learning". National Research Council's Centre for Education, Irvine, California, US, 6–8 Feb 2005

Shulman LS, Quinlan KM (1996) The comparative psychology of school subjects. In: Berliner DC, Calfee RC (eds) Handbook of educational psychology. Macmillan, London

Silva E, Warde A (2010) The importance of Bourdieu. In: Silva E, Warde A (eds) Cultural analysis and Bourdieu's legacy: settling accounts and developing alternatives. Routledge, Abingdon

Smeby J-C (1996) Disciplinary differences in university teaching. Stud High Educ 21:69–79. https://doi.org/10.1080/0307507961233 1381467

Smith W, Tinning R (2011) It's not about logic, it's about logics of practice: a case study of teacher education reform in New Zealand. Asia-Pac J Teach Educ 39(3):235–246. https://doi.org/10.1080/1359866X.2011.588309

United Nations Educational, Scientific and Culture Organization (UNESCO) (2012) Building skills for work and life. In: 3rd UNESCO TVET congress, Shanghai, 16 May 2012

van Oers B (1998) The fallacy of decontextualization. Mind Cult Act 5(2):143–152

Verloop N, Van Driel J, Meijer P (2001) Teacher knowledge and the knowledge base of teaching. Int J Educ Res 35(5):441–461. https://doi.org/10.1016/S0883-0355(02)00003-4

Wellington J (2015) Educational research: contemporary issues and practical approaches. Bloomsbury, London

Williams M, Vogt WP (2014) (eds) The SAGE handbook of innovation in social research methods. Sage, London

Winch C (2014) Know-how and knowledge in the professional curriculum. In: Young M, Muller J (eds) Knowledge, expertise and the professions. Routledge, Abingdon

Wolf A (2015) Issues and ideas: heading for the precipice: can further and higher education funding policies be sustained? The Policy Institute at King's College, London, June 2015 report. Accessed Feb 2016. www.kcl.ac.uk/sspp/policy-institute/publications/Issuesandideasalison-wolf-digital.pdf

Chapter 3
A Comparison of Occupational Education of Teacher Educators' Knowledge and Pedagogy

Abstract This chapter further develops the research monograph on the further education (FE) teacher educators (Loo in Professional development of teacher educators in further education: pathways, knowledge, identities, and vocationalism. Routledge, Abingdon, 2020). It uses the empirical evidence from the project of 33 teacher educators in the sector from FE colleges, higher education institutions and private providers. The chapter seeks to discuss the theoretical frameworks/literature sources of teacher educators' pedagogic (i.e., teaching and learning) activities from the curriculum formation stage to the choice of teaching strategies/approaches. It also compares the types of knowledge and pedagogy of the deliverers in three different teaching settings (i.e., teacher educators working in FE colleges, universities and the private sector) in teacher training/education. The findings will offer the FE community a deep understanding of the commonalities and differences between these three types of educators. This distinct inquiry will provide further scholarly agency to this under-researched topic.

Keywords Teacher educators · Occupational education · Pedagogy · Further education · Knowledge · FE colleges · Higher education institutions/universities · Private providers

Introduction

This chapter investigates the lamentably under-researched teacher educators' knowledge/know-how and pedagogy in the further education (FE) sector. Researchers in the compulsory sectors such as Bullock (2009), Goodwin et al. (2014), Goodwin and Kosnik (2013), Mayer et al. (2011), Swart et al. (2017) and Zeichner (2007) have studied the know-how and pedagogy of this group of educators. An epistemological approach is used. And knowledge is considered a prerequisite to a teacher educator's pedagogic activities.

© The Author(s), under exclusive license to Springer Nature Switzerland AG 2024
S. Loo, *Teaching, Occupational and Further Education*,
https://doi.org/10.1007/978-3-031-67291-0_3

An explanation of the FE sector in England is unnecessary since this has been included in the previous chapter. However, one must remember the sector's characteristics in understanding this discussion.

This chapter aims to discuss the theoretical frameworks/literature sources of teacher educators' pedagogic (i.e., teaching and learning) activities from the curriculum formation stage to the choice of teaching strategies/approaches. The other aim is to investigate the forms of know-how from the three settings: FE colleges, universities and private providers of these educationists.

The chapter is structured in six sections to achieve the aims. The introduction in this first section provides an overview of this chapter, and the literature review offers a circumscribed account of the pertinent sources leading to a theoretical framework. The third section gives the salient details of the related project. The fourth section features the findings. In the next section on discussion, using re-analysed empirical data, it delineates the variations of teacher educators' know-how and pedagogy across the three teaching settings. The conclusion section summarises this chapter.

Review of Relevant Literature Sources

This section delineates a circumscribed account of the relevant literature sources culminating in a conceptual framework. Page 55 of the book (Loo 2020) provides a visual image of this framework and offers a structure for a theoretical discussion. The corresponding chapter—Chap. 5—offers a detailed explanation of the related theories (Loo 2020).

This section has the following areas: (1) defining this group of educators, (2) starting with their know-how from an epistemological standpoint, (3) critiquing the knowledge base, and (4) delineating the knowledge application for pedagogic activities.

Koster et al. (2005, p. 157) view a teacher educator "as someone who provides instruction or who gives guidance and support to student teachers, and who thus renders a substantial contribution to the development of students into competent teachers." Loughran and Berry (2005, p. 307) explicate further Koster et al.'s definition to cover "a complex role that teacher educators play as models of teaching as well as teaching their students [trainee teachers] about teaching." In his definition of teacher educators, Loo (2007) included geographical and contextual factors. Teacher educators educate "prospective teachers, and prospective teachers in all education sectors irrespective of national boundaries, as it is dependent on contexts, be they education settings (sectoral, or institution-related) or country-related" (Loo 2007, p. 426). Thus, teacher educators offer instruction, guidance, and support to trainee teachers and act as teaching models (dual role) across all education sectors and contextual settings.

Berry (2009) went onto explicate the requirements of the teacher educators' roles as:

The "role of teacher educator demands a focus on knowledge about, and learning of, teaching in new and different ways such that expertise as teacher can have limited applicability in practice as a teacher educator. For instance, many new teacher educators quickly learn that the knowledge they bring (typically in the form of stories, activities, and classroom routines) cannot 'simply' be transferred into the thinking and actions of their student teachers – a situation that often challenges new teacher educators' sense of identity as competent professionals. (Murray and Male 2005)"

Murray and Male (2005) sets up this comparison of knowledge between teacher educators and teachers in the compulsory sectors. Loughran (2009, p. 200) further expands on this difference:

Teaching teaching is about knowing the what, why, and how of practice in sophisticated ways and being able to create pedagogical situations that encourage students of teaching to learn about the problematic nature of teaching and to be comfortable in a world of such uncertainty. This would then be the hallmark of the genuine expertise that underpins the scholarship of teaching and the catalyst for explicating a pedagogy of teacher education.

Loughran was insightful in focusing on the dual roles of teacher educators from Bernstein's (1996) perspectives of the what, why and how and acknowledged the uncertainty of these professionals alongside their more profound pedagogical experiences than teachers. Loughran also provided an American platform for future research in the scholarship of teaching.

The above definitions and epistemological approach to teacher educators' knowledge provide a credible academic platform for delineating the conceptual framework of teacher educators' pedagogic activities. The dual complexity dimension of modelling teaching and teaching trainee teachers by Murray and Male (2005) provides the notions of first- and second-order practitioners (teachers and teacher educators, respectively). Murray and Male's dual complexity refer to the compulsory sectors of primary and secondary schools. This chapter will need to reference the FE sector, with over 70% of teachers/lecturers delivering work-related programmes (Loo 2020). Related to this fact is that the relevant lecturers have occupational experiences in industry-related roles. Here, we refer to Handal's (1999) dual professional approach to comprehending FE teacher educators' pedagogic activities, which overlaps with the dual complexity concept by Murray and Male (2005). These dimensions need to be factored into the eventual conceptual framework.

Regarding the epistemological dimension, Loughran's explicit reference to teacher educators' knowledge connects to Bernstein's (1996) knowledge classification. Relating to this classification, his concept of recontextualization offers an understanding of how knowledge is used in teaching settings.

The third area in discussing the eventual theoretical framework focuses on knowledge base before, finally, delineating the knowledge application. The FE teacher educators' knowledge base may be referred to by critical educationists such as Shulman (1987), Loughran et al. (2003), Verloop et al. (2001), Clandinin (1985), Loo (2012), and Banks et al. (1999).

Shulman (1987) offered the iconic typology of teaching knowledge. The typology covered general pedagogical knowledge (including principles and teaching strategies) and pedagogical content knowledge (combining pedagogy and content). Content knowledge might also refer to the disciplinary knowledge of the subjects that teachers specialise in, such as Mathematics and English. Becher (1994) and Smeby (1996) offered a typology of the disciplines of 'hard pure', 'soft pure', 'hard applied', and 'soft applied'. Shulman's typology also included knowledge of educational contexts, knowledge of learners, and knowledge of academic values.

Loughran et al. (2003) emphasised the tacit/implicit aspect of teaching, and Polanyi (1966) covered the individual and science-related elements of tacit knowledge. Collins (2010) provided a more comprehensive account of tacit know-how to include collective know-how. Nonaka and Takeuchi (1995) further developed the collective know-how to encompass working in business organisations.

Verloop et al. (2001) focused on teachers' practical knowledge, beliefs and cognitive capabilities, and Clandinin (1985) referred to teachers; life experiences in her term, 'personal practical knowledge'. Clandinin's approach was further developed by Loo (2012) to include FE teachers' occupational practices and experiences. This development focused on FE's characteristics, which the other researchers omitted as they were concerned with compulsory education. Banks et al. (1999, p. 95) described this type of knowledge as a "complex amalgam of past knowledge, experiences of learning, a personal view of what constitutes 'good' teaching and belief". For this chapter, teaching knowledge is explicit, implicit/tacit, cognitive, practical, and pedagogy-occupation-life-related experiences.

Turning to teacher educators' know-how, Swennen et al. (2008) suggested there were similarities and differences in teachers' knowledge. Teacher educators require more extensive know-how (such as subject areas, learners, pedagogical know-how and approaches that trainee teachers acquire, apply and develop strategies for their professional development) than teachers. Smith (2005) indicated that teacher educators must explain the implicit teaching practice elements to trainee teachers. Goodwin and Kosnik (2013), following Shulman's (1987) idea, provided a typology of five domains of knowledge for (novice) teacher educators. They are personal knowledge (i.e., autobiography and philosophy of teaching), contextual knowledge (understanding of learners, schools and society), pedagogical knowledge (such as content, theories, teaching methods and curriculum development), sociological knowledge (covering diversity, cultural relevance and social justice), and social knowledge (including cooperative, democratic group process and conflict resolution).

Nonaka and Takeuchi (1995), Clarke and Winch (2004) and Eraut (2004) discussed the knowledge, experiences, abilities and skillsets needed for work/occupational practices. Again, a detailed delineation of these sources is located in Chap. 5 (Loo 2020).

Having set out the related theories on the knowledge base of teacher educators, I will turn to its application before finally mapping out the theoretical framework. Acknowledging knowledge, as discussed above, as a prerequisite to a conceptual framework is helpful. However, there needs to be a credible academic connection between knowledge/know-how, as defined in this chapter, and its application for teaching. One approach is Bernstein's vertical and horizontal knowledge classification and his recontextualization concept. The concept means vertical (i.e., explicit and codifiable) knowledge is modified through selection, relocation and refocus in a different educational context (Bernstein 1996). Researchers of occupational education who developed these Bernsteinian theories include van Oers (1998), Barnett (2006), Evans et al. (2010) and Loo (2012, 2014, 2020). Moreover, they covered a broader concept of vertical knowledge and more than one type of recontextualization. Specifically, Evans et al. (2010) offered four types of recontextualization. These included content recontextualization, pedagogic recontextualization, learner recontextualization and workplace recontextualization. Loo (2014, 2020) added three new ones: ongoing recontextualization, occupational recontextualization and integrated applied recontextualization alongside a broader definition of know-how covering knowledge (disciplinary and educational), experiences (occupational, teaching and life), abilities/capabilities and skillsets.

The relevant knowledge-centred concepts to understand how know-how is applied to teaching and learning include (in chronological order) 'logic of practice' (Bourdieu 1992), 'signature pedagogies' (Shulman 2005), 'systems 1 and 2' (Kahneman 2012), 'practice architecture' (Kemmis and Green 2013), and 'knowledgeable practice' (Evans 2016).

The 'logic of practice' concept (Bourdieu 1992) views logic applied in action and solvable using theoretical and practical logic. Pertinent to this approach is context related, and one that emerges "from experience is consistent with the argument that habitus is objectivist" (Lau 2004, p. 376). Shulman's (2005) 'signature of practice' offers three types: uncertainty, engagement, and formation. With a pedagogy of uncertainty, the teacher's responses depend on the learners' reactions to one another and the teacher's adaptations. Learners and teachers need to engage for learning to occur, and 'formation;' refers to building identity, character, dispositions and values. Kahneman's (2012) 'systems 1 and 2' provides two types of decision-making processes, one based on intuition and the other on rational and cognitive interactions. Kemmis and Green's (2013) 'practice architecture' focuses on teachers' sayings, doings and relatings in their pedagogic settings. Evans' (2016) 'knowledgeable practice' centres on formal and informal workplace learning through facilitative structures such as mentoring, coaching and peer learning.

Using the above literature, we can delineate the conceptual framework (Fig. 3.1). The framework used the 'second-order practitioners' concept by Murray and Male (2005) and Handal's (1999) idea of the dual professional approach to create three tiers/dimensions of practices. The top tier refers to teacher educators' practices, i.e., teacher education; the middle tier, teaching practice; and the third tier, occupational practice. The third tier relates to FE teacher educators with previous occupational experiences (e.g., health and social care and engineering).

Reading this framework from left to right, each level/tier, for explanatory purposes, starts with the knowledge source and its acquisition before its application and ends with teaching practice.

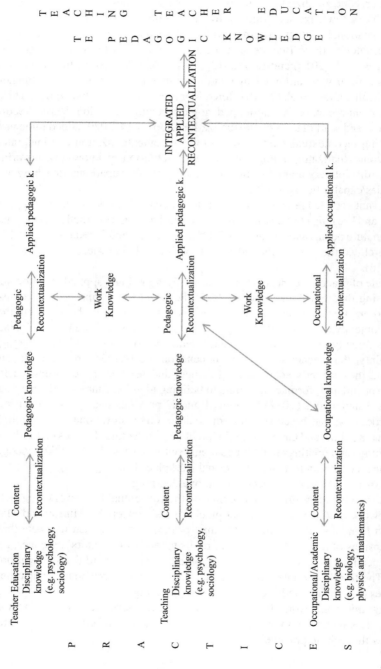

Fig. 3.1 A conceptual framework of (further education) teacher educators' (TE) pedagogic activities

The top tier of teacher educators' practice uses disciplinary/academic knowledge, such as psychology, sociology and business management learning theories. These might be acquired via explicit means (e.g., textbooks) (Shulman 1987; Goodwin and Kosnik 2013). For a visual representation of the major learning theories and their relationships, please refer to Theories of Learning, http://ioe.academia.edu/SaiLoo. However, this know-how is generic. Moreover, it needs to be recontextualized to fit the pedagogic purposes of the teacher educator. Thus, content recontextualization is required (Evans et al. 2010; Loo 2020). After the chosen learning theories are relocated for the teacher educator's purpose, the modified knowledge becomes pedagogic knowledge. This practice stage is related to curriculum development, and the modified know-how needs to apply to teaching (Doyle 1992; Doyle and Rosemartin 2012). The teacher educator's pedagogic knowledge needs to undergo another process with work knowledge. This process is pedagogic recontextualization (Evans et al. 2010; Loo 2020). The combined and modified know-how is then helpful for classroom teaching. Work knowledge refers to the teacher educator's institutional systems, protocols, values and visions (Shulman 1987; Goodwin and Kosnik 2013). The modified know-how becomes applied pedagogic knowledge. This process may involve know-how that is explicit (e.g., disciplinary knowledge), tacit (e.g., personal practical knowledge), experiences (e.g., occupational), abilities (e.g., patience and ability to listen), and skillsets (e.g., intrapersonal and interpersonal) (Shulman 1987; Loughran et al. 2003; Verloop et al. 2001; Clandinin 1985; Loo 2020; Banks et al. 1999). This pedagogic recontextualization process may involve decision-making and professional judgement. The application concepts, such as 'logic of practice' (Bourdieu 1992), 'signature pedagogies' (Shulman 2005), 'systems 1 and 2' (Kahneman 2012), 'practice architecture' (Kemmis and Green 2013), and 'knowledgeable practice' (Evans 2016), will be helpful in understanding how teacher educators perform their roles.

The middle-tier practice of teachers is explained using a similar format as the earlier tier. Before becoming teacher educators, teachers also use disciplinary knowledge such as learning theories (Shulman 1987; Goodwin and Kosnik 2013). The generic know-how needs to undergo content recontextualization (Evans et al. 2010; Loo 2020) to refocus this know-how in readiness to be in a curriculum (Doyle and Rosemartin 2012). The modified know-how or pedagogic knowledge is selected and refocused for a teaching session. This process is pedagogic recontextualization with the teacher's work knowledge (Evans et al. 2020; Loo 2020). The latter know-how refers to the teacher's institutional systems, protocols, values and visions (Shulman 1987; Goodwin and Kosnik 2013). Like in the teacher educator's earlier tier, the related know-how might include explicit, tacit experiences, abilities and skillsets (Shulman 1987; Loughran et al. 2003; Verloop et al. 2001; Clandinin 1985; Loo 2020; Banks et al. 1999). This applied pedagogic knowledge is ready for classroom teaching. The application concepts espoused earlier would be pertinent in understanding how teachers carry out their teaching.

The final tier refers to the occupational practice, i.e., teachers with occupational experiences in their disciplines, such as health and social care and engineering. As explained in the earlier tiers, they need to acquire specialized knowledge. However, there might be instances where the teacher educators and teachers did not have occupational experiences. These might include academics of 'hard pure' (e.g., Zoology) and 'soft pure' (e.g., Philosophy) disciplines (Becher 1994). irrespective of whether the practitioners have occupational or academic know-how, their generic knowledge needs to undergo content recontextualization (Evans et al. 2010; Loo, 2020). Again, this is part of the curriculum development in any taught programme. Practitioners who eventually become teachers or teacher educators modify their know-how to become occupational knowledge. [The modified knowledge may be known as recontextualized academic subject knowledge for those eventually teaching academic subjects (e.g., mathematics and physics). This knowledge is used for teaching (middle tier) in the pedagogic recontextualization process.] Those practitioners (before becoming teachers or teacher educators) will then use their occupational knowledge with work knowledge (as defined in the previous two tiers) to relocate the know-how via occupational recontextualization (Evans et al. 2020; Loo 2020). The know-how maybe explicit, tacit experiences, abilities and skillsets (Nonaka and Takeuchi 1995; Clarke and Winch 2004; Eraut 2004). The changed know-how is known as applied occupational knowledge. Again, the application concepts stated earlier would offer a greater understanding of how these practitioners use their modified know-how in their work practices.

We now have three types of applied pedagogic knowledge from teacher education, teaching and occupation practices. The know-how is needed to apply in classroom settings; it needs to undergo a final process of integrated applied recontextualization. With the know-how, the teacher educator can choose the appropriate teaching strategy for the specific session at a particular academic level for her/his learners (i.e., teacher trainees) and from a part of the curriculum. This nuanced and complicated framework results from the complex roles of FE teacher educators. Their roles include

- teaching trainees how to be teachers,
- modelling good practice via their extensive pedagogic experiences as teacher educators and teachers, and
- incorporating these experiences in their complex activities for those educators with occupational practices.

This literature review section started by defining teacher educators. It argued the relevance of knowledge (teacher educators') from an epistemological viewpoint. The delineation of the three-tier conceptual framework of FE teacher educators' activities was in two stages: the knowledge base and knowledge application culminating in the final process: integrated applied recontextualization to enable teacher educators to choose the appropriate teaching strategy.

The framework is dynamic and non-directional, even though the discussion started from the left (knowledge sources and acquisition relating to curriculum development) to the right (knowledge application to teaching strategies) across the three tiers. Thus, a teacher with occupational practice and experience might practice in an FE setting without qualifying as a teacher. It is not unusual in the FE sector, unlike the compulsory sector, as occupational teachers start teaching without having a teaching qualification initially. In this case, the content recontextualization process would be missed in the middle-tier teaching practice. The content recontextualization stage can be achieved by qualifying as a trained teacher. In rare cases, as indicated by one of the participants, a teacher educator practised as one before formally completing a higher academic qualification. Here, one assumes that an educator requires a higher qualification (after the formal teacher training to practise as a teacher). This higher qualification offers further educational know-how that can be relocated (via content recontextualization) in the curriculum development stage. In short, this unique framework provides a deeper understanding of how an FE teacher educator acquires and applies the necessary know-how in training trainee teachers.

Project Details

There were eight research volunteers in this unfunded project. They are the Principal Investigator (PI), Dr. Sai Loo (University College London), and the Co-investigators (CI), Dr. Gordon Ade-Ojo (University of Greenwich), Heather Booth-Martin (Craven College), Dr. John Bostock (Edge Hill University), Dr. Jim Crawley (Bath Spa University), Baiba Eberte (Carlton Training), Nicola Sowe (NBS Teacher Training, Professional Development and Consultancy), and Sonia Spencer (North Hertfordshire College). The investigators had experiences as teacher educators in the sector. They worked in different work settings of higher education institutions, further education colleges and private providers using other teacher education-related specifications. The ethical committee of the PI's institution approved the project before the start of this project. The related research question in this chapter is what knowledge(s) do they (i.e., teacher educators) draw upon and apply in their work?

The targeted participants were teacher educators in the post-compulsory/lifelong learning sector who had volunteered to be PI, CIs or participants via approaches from CIs. The PI made an initial call for co-researchers to the following national networks: TELL, Learning and Skills Research Network (LSRN), and British Educational Research Association (BERA).

The research methodologies included a range of quantitative and qualitative research methods. The methods included a survey/questionnaire, one-to-one semi-structured interviews, documentary research and 'Talking Heads'. A questionnaire survey was used to elicit quantitative data such as gender, age group, academic qualifications, teaching experiences as an educator and a teacher, and occupational and relevant life experiences. Interviews were used to capture rich textured data on the interviewees' journeys to be teacher educators, the nature of their work, relevant pedagogic knowledge, and its application and perceptions of themselves as teacher educators. Documentary research included relevant government reports and programme specifications. "Talking heads" were digital audio recordings of the participants' narratives of being and becoming teacher educators. The Talking Head recordings provided a sense of ownership and means of professional identification for the participants. The participants in this project included all the investigators (PI and CIs) and additional colleagues, and the purposive sample of the project totalled

33. These audio recordings were anonymized to safeguard personal and institutional information and prevent identifying specific individuals. A pilot study from the group of CIs fine-tuned the research instruments proposed in this project. The agreed guidelines for the researchers as participants were issued to enable an ethical approach to participate in this project. The data analysis, such as the questionnaire, was carried out by a small group drawn from the eight co-investigators. The PI used an audit trail approach of linking (a) a participant's captured details of their completed survey, interview, and Talking Head recordings, and (b) seeking commonalities between the analysed data from each of the three data sources. This two-pronged approach was applied in analysing, synthesizing, and detailing the relevant data for use in the contributions in this research monograph. The details of the analysed findings relating to specific participants were made anonymous. In this chapter, the data of the teacher educators' know-how is re-analysed regarding the three teaching settings of FE colleges, universities and private providers.

Findings

This section offers the readers a critical delineation of FE teacher educators' know-how (types and application to pedagogic activities) from the perspectives of those educators in FE colleges, universities and private providers. These three perspectives will offer a logical discussion under each of the three parts. However, it is not always possible to order the knowledge types and applications sequentially as they may be intricately connected. A discussion section subsequently follows.

The purposive empirical data relating to this chapter comprised 32 teacher educators who participated in the questionnaire and one-to-one interviews: 15 from FE colleges, 13 from HEIs, and four from private providers.

FE Colleges

> 'Knowledge' is derived from numerous sources which include the family and wider society. Each teacher-trainer already has a view of teaching, based on personal experience. Learning about FE ITE pedagogy is part of the job. The teacher-educator teaches pedagogy, at the same time developing her/his own understanding. Learning comes from reading, CPD, colleagues, ITE students, study and research.

> ITE 'Knowledge' is applied by the teacher-educator in classroom delivery through lectures, group work, pair work, mentoring, coaching and assessment of assignments. The teacher-educator already has her/his own 'discipline' or 'vocational subject' such as a B.Sc., B.A. or B.Ed. He/she is also teacher-trained; for example, has the PGCE or Cert Ed. The teacher trainer transfers practitioner skills and knowledge to the ITE classroom. Trainee teachers learn from study and assignments; but, also from the teacher-educator who acts as a 'role model'. For example, how to manage a classroom can be demonstrated by changing the layout each week.

Findings

Teacher-educator 'forms of knowledge' are the same as those used by teachers/lecturers, as already indicated. However there a greater range is required because the trainee-teacher cohort is so varied. Groups are 'mixed ability', mixed age, mixed 'discipline' and 'skill'. An FE ITE group is likely to be made up of some students educated to no more than QCF3 ('A' level/NVQ3) in their 'vocational area' to some with Doctorates (QCF8) in their specific 'discipline'. All have equal status and equal needs as trainee teachers. (TE33, Interview, p. 2)

I try and model good practice for my trainees. You are sending out a message to them. When I was teaching 16 years old students [in hospitality], I wasn't modelling in the same way. It was more about the subject content...I refer to my knowledge from my teaching experiences...I have to say that this [PGCE] programme is a generic course, which includes all subjects that trainees teach on, but then what does that mean being a generic course? (TE6, Interview, p. 2)

You can only be a TE if you understand what goes on in classrooms. It would help if you also were good at what you do in the classrooms, for example, managing classroom behaviour. The learners need to know that they are getting a good deal. As a TE, it is vital to be well-organised and have good planning, letting learners understand where they are in their journey and how well they are doing. As a TE, you must deal with a trainee's view of what makes a good teacher. Sometimes that can be clouded by their own experience of what they think is a good teacher. Therefore, TEs need to help them understand how to make a good class, and it needs to be realised in the idea of being a good teacher...I describe knowledge as coming from experience – own and past experience, a currency of knowledge linked to qualifications and from the government's point of view and how it impinges upon us as a teacher. I don't believe that anyone can come into being a TE unless they have knowledge of working classrooms and changing classrooms – changes in the student grouping and the range of abilities found in a classroom. I have seen some classrooms where there is a range of abilities which I'm not sure who that would be good for. Where you have level 2 and 3 students in one class, you ask who is being 'taught' at what time in the session...In good classrooms, all teachers work from the same basis – their knowledge over the years, current knowledge and future knowledge. As technology is used in the classroom, I'm not always convinced if it is used for learning or has got to be used...The functional skill of English needs the most attention. English language in the classroom is poor in some situations. Teachers are in a difficult situation as they have to teach the basics of English. It is due to school children being allowed to drop English at 14. Every course should have an English language unit and make it an intrinsic and explicit part of any course. TE should have an English, Maths and ICT unit on the programme despite being found in the minimum core. It needs to be stronger. (TE13, Interview, p. 2)

Knowledge divided into 'practical know-how' and 'theoretical knowledge' so we know why we do things. This job is intuitive, but we need a theoretical base such as theory to 'marry practice' how theoretical knowledge work in practice. Examples are learning styles: I first thought there was a lot of sense in the principles but trusted it less as I used it more. When the ideas were critically examined in the Coffield et al. (2004) study, it was shown how approaches to learning styles were making organizations money but not having a significant beneficial impact on learning. (TE16, Interview, p. 2)

[Knowledge] comes from reading and research and my personal and professional learning networks on social media and the community of practice. A complex loop...a number 8 on its side...a continual movement around this...this is praxis. I do something or see/read something and try it out. I was looking into concepts such as neurodiversity, which I gave feedback to learners. Teaching teacher education is a complex relationship between theory and practice. Also, technical knowledge that never goes out of fashion...The scheme of work is strategic. The lesson plan is operational. Technical things are important. Teacher education programmes teach the wrong knowledge. Why are we teaching about dead white male psychologists that have no relevance today? – These educational thinkers are no longer relevant. This is why people think teacher education is crap and it is. We should be teaching Bel Hooks. Why are we still teaching Skinner? Why has no one worked this out? Its dull and boring to them…its endemic even in xxx institution. (TE 23, Interviews, p. 2)

Occupational learning consists of a broad spectrum of subjects in a rich [learning] environment but is difficult to relate directly to the subject. This is when practice and mentor support come into play more. The theoretical approach is to get teachers to look at what they do and question it, but they need to see the practical application. Trainees need to experience the theory and then use it in their practice by 'pick and mix' and apply them. Trainees are encouraged to play with them and have a go and take a risk. (TE25, Interview, p. 2)

I think the teacher's role is to open someone's life to take action. Some are trying to move on into the second question, which is about knowledge and you teach particular aspects of knowledge management and finally skills from a theoretical perspective that a student maybe reluctant to hear. But I think that they need to understand skills and why teaching can go wrong. They need to know about different models and the different theories and not to give them toolkits and not working out why a particular session has not gone right. It is not enough to just provide them with teaching approaches. They need to find out which ones are more valuable during their training.

So, they need to learn social learning theories and to see their development and particularly to know that teaching is much slower and a more subtle process and over time, be more willing to engage with teaching the students concerning your own as you teach the knowledge of various types of practical or theoretical knowledge. You find yourself feeling the particular approaches to knowledge, for particular kinds of knowledge, of specific aspects of knowledge that stand out and what regularly appears to work, what appears to be more relevant than others. Students would reflect this learning series. You see particular ones I think because it great and because of the practical skills are still behavioural. You have got to do this and get you it right. (TE25, Talking Head, p. 1)

A wide range of different knowledge is relevant…reading across and drawing on psychology, anthropology, business, politics, economics, environment and other areas …/drawing in from a wide range as it suits the situation. I link knowledge and theories with practice e.g., in observations. I like to do things differently and vary the activities as I'm always coming at it differently. It's almost like it's new every time, that constant process of addition and change to knowledge. (TE 31, Interviews, p. 2)

Universities

You can't be a teacher educator unless you understand what goes on in classrooms. (TE12, Interview, p. 2)

I didn't think I had sufficient depth of knowledge. I knew the content was on teaching and I had a variety of experiences to draw on as analogies. Knowing how learners learn and how to explain that to trainee teachers using a variety of knowledge were useful. (TE18, Interview, p. 1)

Teacher educators have a much deeper understanding that informs my practice, and I need to keep updating, exploring and reflecting on making me a better teacher. (TE18, Interview, p. 2)

Findings 45

> Occupational and subject knowledge is fundamental. I had a cross-curricula role [as a Lecturer in an HEI and previously as Heads of Department in FE colleges and schools], and I took my own experiences of teaching subject knowledge [in drama] to bring to the classroom. (TE20, Interview, p. 1)

> This [teaching knowledge] is an area that was not talked about when I was a teacher educator at the HEI. It was just assumed that we knew it or perhaps we did not and so we did not discuss it. In any case, looking back at this hazy period, I think knowledge (whichever it is defined) is essential. If we do not know what it is, how do we convey that professionalism as a teacher educator?
>
> The forms of knowledge are similar to being a teacher. They include theories of learning and teaching and those by the social constructivists, and behaviourists. These might be termed educational (education related as these concepts are borrowed from other disciplines such as psychology, management and sociology) theories. Researchers like Clandinin, Shulman, and Verloop et al. focused on teaching knowledge for the compulsory sectors, and these could be adapted for FE. Alongside this pedagogic knowledge, some might be explicit or codified and others, tacit. For example, Clandinin uses the term, 'personal practical knowledge' of teachers where their knowledge maybe based on their experiences - pedagogic or life - and this allows tacit forms of pedagogic knowledge to be included. Collins, Nonaka and Takeuchi and Polanyi offer different varieties of tacit knowledge, and these have influences on how we view pedagogic knowledge. (TE21, Interview, p. 2–3)

> I draw on content knowledge [linguist teacher in German, French and Spanish] with an underpinning theory as part of the art of pedagogy. Perhaps, more importantly, are my own life experiences and when learning how to teach Modern Foreign Languages. In the first lesson, I realised that students wanted to learn and not catch teachers out. Those experiences are important, and I bring them in. Also, I was a performer for a short time, and I realised I could sway the masses. I never made the audience or one individual a laughing-stock. I was the one who was laughed at and never humiliate them. I bring this into my teaching and teacher training. I help them to understand that they can do better. (TE7, Interview, p. 2)

> We accumulate a great deal of experience and knowledge, but it is the experience that is important. From research in this area [where he gained a Ph.D.], it recognizes that there are several theories/knowledges that informs our practice and not just one or two that rule the roost. If someone is trying to put one view forward, that doesn't interest me very much. I draw upon knowledge from different sources and link this to actual practice. Making connections between what you discuss and help [trainee] teachers to understand what the underpinning theory of knowledge is connected to that practice. Thus, making these connections is crucial to practice. (TE9, Interviews, p. 2)

> To be a TE, you need to have experience in a full teaching role, i.e. teaching a class for a few years and knowing the students; having a pastoral role requires being very good at admin (tracking students). I got that from my admin programme experience as I am very organized. I would prepare my lesson a week in advance and put them in a filing cabinet so that I didn't have to worry and could make last-minute changes to manage my time and stress levels. I think being a good TE; one should be able to show trainees how to organize themselves to minimize their stress. You also need, as a TE to know the difference between pedagogy and andragogy and managing learning environments to minimize problems – the psychology of classrooms (went on to talk about managing students on certain bad days). I was used, e.g., to working with trainees at the start of a course when they were immersed in discussions, by ringing a bell and they stopped talking (e.g. to show behaviourism is not dead!). If you can build into your sessions models of learning and linking to theories of learning, and reflect, and if one is teaching a lot, it's challenging to find time to do that. Also, observe others'

teaching. I saw a lot of films about education in French and English and became obsessive about how people teach. As TE, we are constantly learning and modelling them. It would help if you were an expert teacher first in all its dimensions (assessment, group work etc.) and knowing your strengths and weaknesses and your students (esp. teenagers) so you get used to their moods. You can teach the same way to two different cohorts and still get it wrong, so in a sense, it may seem common sense, but as a TE, we know about the learning theories, and these are not our ideas, but able to use these. For TE and teachers, it is most important to collaborate to get ideas from each other and to network to learn from each other. Creating a climate of trust and TE tends to share opinions/resources that perhaps teachers may not want to do. It doesn't matter as these teaching strategies are applied in different contexts, so it is not stealing. The issue is time. (TE12, Interview, p. 1)

I remember thinking I couldn't do this on my own. I don't think you can be a good TE if you don't have at least a good mentor, as you don't know what you don't know. A good mentor maintains your confidence and shows you what you need to improve and how to do it… TE needs more depth and breadth (expanded on salient e.gs. incl. .in a safe environment) and has to be more familiar with learning theories and the RSA and neuroscience report and critique theories. Teachers need breadth and depth in terms of learning theories. TEs need a level of confidence, which comes from having a more profound and broader knowledge base for their credibility, authority and authenticity. And if you don't know it, say so, as one is not expected to know everything, but you can inspire people to learn more about their topic of interest. I enjoyed my MA in mentoring; as a TE, they [TEs] should also be role model mentors. (TE12, Interview, p. 2)

Private Providers

[Referring to different types of knowledge for work] these included, e.g., communication to help people to understand, plan courses and lessons, understand the purpose of the [teacher training] qualification, understand why learners struggle, comply with policies, design teaching materials and help me when I am stuck and need support. (TE11, Questionnaire, no. 10)

I have worked for a few years and have seen quite a lot. It helps me immensely in trying to tailor my teaching to the needs of my learners. But if there is one thing specific about teacher training, the knowledge I have accumulated over the years could not be learnt; I do not think in any other way. From experience, I have met so many interesting people coming from very diverse backgrounds. I have learnt so much about different industries in the UK, where people who attended my courses ended up teaching and training afterwards. So, the knowledge I use in my teaching is the everyday knowledge I have learnt as I have worked and lived in the UK. The experiences I have had back in Latvia, especially working at the schools, were more to do with organisational skills and planning skills, but maybe not so much about how to deal with people, handle people, and manage people in the classroom because our cultures are different. I think that things work differently in Latvia. My experiences when teaching adults English in England are those experiences that I can use because I had people from different backgrounds, people from different social circles, age groups and others. I sometimes rely on those experiences. I have all these things to help me to be a teacher educator. (TE11, Talking Head, p. 2)

I teach AET, and I am involved in the delivery and assessment of CET and DET programmes. I need to have knowledge of the subject, which is teaching background, and maybe it is not correct to say, "practical knowledge", but you need to have pedagogical and methodological

Discussion 47

knowledge. It is a bit difficult to explain but to give you an example, if it were about teaching the Polish language, I would need to understand how the language works and how to pass the information on to others, which comes under methodology.

I also use the knowledge of presenting information based on my experience because everything comes with time and practice. If you are inexperienced, you tend to rely on the theory; however, with time, you see that things work differently from how they were explained to you. Teaching experience is a crucial source of knowledge that I use in my role. I am now a more effective teacher than at the start of my career. I have improved due to my experiences and preparation. But I have also tried to read about some topics to learn more.

However, being able to teach doesn't just come from experience. I first learnt to teach during the education that I received. I studied how to teach at the university and went to schools where we had teaching practice. Once we acquired knowledge, we were asked to go and implement it. It all started with me studying the subject and then practising it.

In terms of how I apply my knowledge in my current role, let me give you an example of providing feedback to learners, which is one of the topics I cover with my students. When I was studying to become a teacher, giving feedback was covered in the lectures, which is how I learnt about it. Then, when I was teaching Polish, I provided feedback to my learners. So now I have got it in my head, and I can explain this to others.

A teacher educator should be knowledgeable about the practical nature of teaching and the nitty gritty of teaching techniques because this is their subject matter. Teachers of other subjects will have their subject matter. However, I can only imagine a teacher educator with experience teaching different topics. Like in my case, when I was teaching Polish, I could practise what I teach now. I don't think I would be successful without this experience. I learnt from my students as well. For example, when I was teaching at schools in Poland, I taught in primary school and then in secondary school, which I found more stimulating. They made me work quite hard. Then in the UK, I started teaching adults, so I have more than ten years of teaching experience.

My cultural background and experiences abroad do not affect me as a teacher very much because the principles of teaching and the methods are the same. I would teach there in the same way I do here (TE24, Interview, p. 1–2). ...knowledge of my subject, strategies, learning and teaching techniques taught in my subject [Polish] link theory and practice. (TE24, Talking Heads, p. 1)

Discussion

This discussion sector starts by positing the above relevant empirical data to the theoretical framework and then delineating the commonalities and differences of knowledge types and applications across the three sectors.

Theoretical Framework

It is overwhelmingly evident that knowledge is a prerequisite to teaching and, in this study, to teacher educators, such as the TEs 6, 7, 9, 11, 12, 13, 16, 17, 18,

20, 21, 23, 24, 25, 31, and 33. The sources and types as illustrated by the above narratives are diverse. The related researchers include Shulman (1987), Clandinin (1985), Nonaka and Takeuchi (1995), Bernstein (1996), Banks et al. (1999), Verloop, van Driel and Meijer (2001), Loughran et al. (2003), Clarke and Winch (2004), Eraut (2004), Smith (2005), Swennen et al. (2008), Loo (2012), and Goodwin and Kosnik (2013). TE33 explains, "Each teacher-trainer already has a view of teaching based on personal experience. Learning about FE ITE pedagogy is part of the job. The teacher-educator teaches pedagogy, at the same time developing her/his own understanding. Learning comes from reading, CPD, colleagues, ITE students, study and research". This constant learning process alights with Loo's (2014) ongoing recontextualization.

However, the know-how is conflated to cover teacher educators, teachers and occupational practitioners. One of the aims of this investigation is to classify and delineate the know-how into the three practices of the theoretical framework: teacher education, teaching and occupations.

With the teacher education practice dimension, content know-how may be acquired through initial teacher education qualifications, reading, continuous professional development (CPD), colleagues, and research, as exemplified by TE 33. TE 24 suggested that "a teacher educator should be knowledgeable about the practical nature of teaching and the nitty gritty of teaching techniques because this is their subject matter." This narrative is insightful as it situates the unspecified and tacit aspects of a teacher educator's curriculum. However, there are the generic teaching qualification specifications of the Learning and Skills Improvement Services (LSIS) (2013). Furthermore, there was a scant attempt to define or typologize knowledge (Loo 2018), let alone relate to teacher educators. Content knowledge for teacher educators would include theories of learning and teaching (as for teachers).

Of course, this content knowledge of teacher educators is generic. It needs to undergo a content recontextualization process to relocate it to a specific context for a teacher educator's use. The modified pedagogic knowledge is then further changed via pedagogic recontextualization. This second process also includes work knowledge relating to the teaching institution of the teacher educator. Examples include TEs 33 and 12 mentioning the relevance of being mentored as teacher educators at their workplaces. TE12 explained the importance of creating a climate of trust in the teaching workplace and being able to share opinions and resources. Examples of using 'pedagogic knowledge' included planning courses and lessons, understanding the purpose of the [teacher education] qualification, understanding why teacher trainees struggle, complying with policies, and designing teaching materials (TE11). TE12 suggested that being very organised in administrating the teacher education programme (to minimise stress) and having the ability to manage learning environments and model learning and teaching were helpful. TE12 suggested that being confident arose from a "more profound and broader knowledge base."

The above modified pedagogic knowledge of teacher educators, i.e., applied pedagogic knowledge is ready for the final process. However, this final stage requires the modified know-how of the other two practices: teaching and occupation.

Discussion 49

The teaching practice dimension undergoes the two recontextualization processes as above. Content recontextualization could refer to the 'discipline of teaching', such as learning theories (TE16). This know-how can then be relocated for specific teaching via pedagogic recontextualization. This process requires two types of know-how. They are pedagogic knowledge (via content recontextualization) and work knowledge. These knowledge forms may be explicit or tacit and are related to the teachers' work settings. The modified know-how becomes applied pedagogic knowledge and is ready for the final process.

The final occupational practice also undergoes two processes. Content recontextualization involves disciplinary knowledge, which TE33 described as discipline or vocational subject know-how. TE6 called it subject content. TE20 viewed occupational and subject knowledge as fundamental at this curriculum formation/development stage (Doyle 1992; Doyle and Rosemartin 2012). The changed/relocated knowledge, i.e., occupational knowledge, is ready to be used in a specific occupational context. The occupational recontextualization process enables the occupational content and work knowledge (such as IT system, organizational protocols, and mentoring system) to be relocated in readiness to apply the know-how to specific work situations. This modified know-how is called applied occupational knowledge.

All three forms of applied know-how from teacher education, teaching and occupational practices can now be relocated for 'classroom' teaching via the Integrated Applied Recontextualization (IAR) process. These applications involve decision-making in choosing the appropriate teaching strategies for a particular cohort at a specific academic level (Bourdieu 1992; Shulman 2005; Kahneman 2012; Kemmis and Green 2013; Evans 2016). Various metaphors and phrases were used to describe this complex stage. TE23 described this as a complex loop, like a number 8 on its side. For TE31, it was the linking of knowledge and theories with practice. TE24 included her cultural background and experiences, knowledge of her subject strategies, and learning and teaching techniques taught in her subject [Polish], linking theory and practice. She further delineates her journey: "being able to teach does not just come from experience. I first learnt to teach during the education that I received. I studied how to teach at the university and went to schools where we had teaching practice. Once we acquired knowledge, we were asked to go and implement it. It all started with me studying the subject and then practising it".

The above brief delineation using the empirical evidence and relating to the conceptual framework offers insights into the conflated, complex, and dynamic interactions of the diverse forms of know-how via teacher educators' acquisition and application processes.

Commonalities and Differences Across the Three Sectors

In this section on the three teaching settings of FE colleges, universities and private providers, the re-analysed empirical data is divided into two parts: similarities and differences, and in each of the parts, four themes: knowledge types, knowledge applications, attributes and miscellaneous.

Similarities

Regarding knowledge types, the teacher educators from the three teaching settings acknowledge and typologize the know-how. From educators in FE colleges, terms such as 'wide range' (TE31) and 'greater range' (TE33) were indicated. Other ones from those teaching in universities included 'much deeper understanding that informs my practice' (TE18) and 'more depth and breadth' (TE12).

For teacher educators in FE colleges, the range of knowledge types and sources included reading and disciplines such as psychology, anthropology, etc. (TE31). TE33 mentioned families and wider society, personal experiences, continuous professional development sessions, colleagues, trainee teachers, study, research and discipline or vocational subject knowledge. TE33 further indicated knowledge from practitioner skills. For TE13, knowledge may come from experiences, qualifications, government policies, and from learners. TE16 distinguished practical and theoretical knowledge as being a teacher educator is intuitive. TE23 emphasised reading, personal and professional learning networks on social media and communities of practice. TE25 viewed occupational learning as a broad spectrum of subjects.

The teacher educators in higher education, such as TE20, felt that occupational and subject knowledge was fundamental as she had a cross-curricula role. She used her experiences of teaching drama (subject knowledge) to bring to the classroom. TE18 thought that she needed more depth of knowledge. But knowledge could include a variety of experiences to draw on as analogies. Also helpful was knowing how learners learn and that a teacher educator needed to keep updating, exploring and reflecting on being a better teacher educator. TE7 drew on his content knowledge as a linguist teacher in German, French and Spanish alongside his life experiences and learning to teach Modern Foreign Languages.

From the private provider teacher educators, TE11's accumulation of knowledge could not be learnt [on a course]. Her life experiences were drawn from meeting interesting people from diverse backgrounds. TE24 indicated the need for subject knowledge, which was teaching background or practical knowledge. She distinguished practical knowledge from pedagogical and methodological knowledge, which she explained as "teaching the Polish language, I would need to understand how the language works and how to pass the information onto others which comes under methodology".

The above types and sources of teacher educators' know-how are diverse. The subject, content, theory, pedagogical and methodological knowledge, and learners' knowledge may be associated with Shulman's (1987) and Goodwin and Kosnik's (2013) findings. Those related experiences could be associated with Clandinin's (1985) and Loo's (2012) findings. The additional explanations of the teacher educators also offer new insights in addition to the literature mentioned above sources as these are specific to this specific group of educationists.

Discussion

Regarding knowledge applications, similar aspects cover their descriptions. In FE colleges, TE33 described her activities as classroom delivery via lectures, group work, mentoring, coaching and assessments, transfer of practitioner skills into the classroom, and role modelling good practice. TE13 emphasized the need to understand what happens in the classroom, including managing behaviour. TE16 suggested marrying theory with practice. TE23 viewed the complex relationship between theory and practice as a complex loop, where "technical knowledge never goes out of fashion", and that schemes of work were strategic and lesson planning, operational. TE25 stressed the need for trainees to experience theory and put it into practice by picking, mixing, applying, and encouraging risk-taking. She saw a teacher's role as opening someone's life to take action. TE31 linked knowledge and theories with practice in observations. For her, it involved a "constant process of addition and change to knowledge". This statement chimed with Loo's (2014) ongoing recontextualization process.

For those teaching in universities, similar sentiments were expressed. TE12 indicated that "you can't be a teacher educator unless you understand what goes on in classrooms". She mentioned teaching sessions as "models of learning and linking to theories of learning"…" and as teacher educators, we constantly learn and model them.

The teacher educators in the private sector provided a practical delineation of a teacher educator's duties. These covered helping learners understand, plan courses and lessons, understand the purpose of the [teacher education] qualification and why learners struggle, comply with policies, and design teaching materials (TE11). For TE24, her role involved being "knowledgeable about the practical nature of teaching and the nitty gritty of teaching techniques because this is their subject matter. Teachers of other subjects will have their subject matter".

Whether taking an abstract or a practical perspective to enact the duties of teacher educators, all the educators in the three teaching settings agree that their work is multifaceted and layered. Those in the private provider sector may approach their roles practically, possibly due to their shorter and often below university-level courses. From the un-representative sample of the project, they have the essential teacher education qualification, not postgraduate qualifications. These factors might account for their more down-to-earth approach, whereas educators in the other two teaching settings offered both a practical and theoretical approach to their roles. Private provider teacher educators subscribe more to Bourdieu's (1992) logic of practice, which was context related. All the teacher educators exhibited aspects of Kemmis and Green's (2013) practice architecture with their articulations and actionable agencies related to their teaching settings. The mentoring and support structures indicated by the teacher educators subscribed to Evan's (2016) knowledgeable practice concept.

The third and last commonality relates to attributes. In particular, TE13 in FE mentioned capabilities such as managing classroom behaviour and organizing and planning abilities. TE12 in a university setting testified to being organized to minimize stress (for both themselves and to show their trainee teachers). TE11 from the private sector subscribed to having communication intelligence to help people to understand and plan courses and lessons. These capabilities, attributes and skill sets are associated with the findings by Nonaka and Takeuchi (1995), Clarke and Winch (2004) and Eraut (2004). However, the capacities above are specific to this group of educationists. Nonaka and Takeuchi's findings centred on workers in large Japanese companies. Clarke and Winch's writings were theoretical. Eraut's research centred on occupations such as Business and Engineering. Nevertheless, the three sources offer this chapter a broader definition of know-how incorporating experiences, capabilities and skill sets.

Differences

Regarding knowledge types, TE23 in FE lamented the 'wrong' kind of knowledge taught in teacher education courses. She questioned why we teach about dead white male psychologists that have no relevance today and argued that people like Bel Hooks would be more relevant than Skinner (TE23). In universities, teacher educators like TE7 used the term 'art of pedagogy', which combined content knowledge (e.g., from German, French and Spanish languages) with underpinning theory to delineate knowledge types and applications. TE9 centred on research to inform his knowledge sources, and TE21 focused on tacit know-how to help him understand his role as a teacher educator. By inference, TE11 in the private provider setting derived her [implicit] experiences from living and working in the UK and Latvia.

Connecting knowledge types and applications, TE12 in a university teaching setting indicated confidence and the ability to be aware of one's strengths and weaknesses and have the intra- and interpersonal intelligence to collaborate with other educators. The capacity to create trust and confidence comes from a more profound and broader knowledge base for one's credibility, authority and authenticity. TE11 from the private sector emphasized the cultural dimension of working and living in the UK and Latvia in helping her deliver her course as a teacher educator. TE24's life and teaching experiences in Poland and the UK do not affect her teaching as a teacher educator because "the principles of teaching and the methods are the same". Lastly, under the miscellaneous theme, both teacher educators in FE provided two issues. TE6 queried the generic nature of her teacher education course where traditionally, subject pedagogy was not emphasized. TE13 centred on the remedial work of FE teachers on delivering the minimum core of English, Mathematics and Information Technology subjects.

The above attributes, tacit know-how, cultural experiences, remedial work offer differences between the themes and teaching settings, even though one might associate them with literature sources such as Nonaka and Takeuchi (1995), Banks et al. (1999), Clarke and Winch (2004), Eraut (2004), Smith (2005), and Collins (2010).

The different issues (i.e., generic nature of the ITE course, inappropriate sources, and remedial work) brought up by FE teacher educators indicate their close insights into the FE sector issues. The varying issues identified by educators teaching in universities provided an overview of a teacher educator's requirements as an educational cohort for research or, perhaps, a greater awareness of an academic cohort. The two teacher educators in the private providers offered different issues concerning international backgrounds that may affect their deliveries judging from their curricula vitae.

Conclusion

This chapter focused on the occupational education of teacher educators' knowledge and pedagogy across the teaching settings of FE colleges, universities and private providers. It used re-analysed empirical evidence (though not necessarily representative) and a conceptual framework of teacher educators' educational activities to understand better this cohort's know-how types, sources and applications. A teacher educator's work is complex and conflated with dynamic interactions of diverse know-how via a teacher educator's acquisition and application processes. Also, the chapter compared teacher educators' knowledge agencies in three teaching settings of FE, universities and private providers. Commonalities of broad knowledge types and sources, including theoretical, disciplinary and educational knowledge, experiences, attributes and skill sets, were found. Analogies and teacher educators' characteristics described the complexities and dynamism of teacher educators' work in marrying theory with practice.

Regarding differences, those teaching in FE offered close insights into the sector. Teacher educators in university settings had a greater sense of their requirements and awareness as a specific educational cohort for possible further studies. Those in the private sector provided a culturally international perspective of their work.

The above insights affect how teacher educators are initially trained and professionally developed. The findings also offer managers and institutions thinking about the requirements of this cohort of educationists. Policymakers need to consider the complexities of the significant work of this under-studied and undervalued group. The conceptual framework and findings offer a new and nuanced understanding of the know-how and its applications of FE teacher educators.

References

Banks F, Leach J, Moon B (1999) New understandings of teachers' pedagogic knowledge. In: Leach J, Moon B (eds) Learners and pedagogy. Paul Chapman Publishing, London

Barnett M (2006) Vocational knowledge and vocational pedagogy. In: Young M, Gamble J (eds) Knowledge, curriculum and qualifications for South African further education. Human Sciences Research Council Press, Cape Town

Becher T (1994) The significance of disciplinary differences. Stud High Educ 19:151–161

Bernstein B (1996) Pedagogy, symbolic control and identity: theory, research, critique. Taylor and Francis Limited, London

Berry A (2009) Professional self-understanding as expertise in teaching about teaching. Teach Teach Theory Pract 15(2):305–318

Bourdieu P (1992) Logic of practice. Polity Press, Bristol

Bullock SM (2009) Learning to think like a teacher educator: making the substantive and syntactic structures of teaching explicit through self-study. Teach Teach Theory Pract 15(2):291–304

Clandinin J (1985) Personal practical knowledge: a study of teachers' classroom images. Curric Inq 15(4):361–385

Clarke L, Winch C (2004) Apprenticeship and applied theoretical knowledge. Educ Philos Theory Incorpor Access 36(5):509–521

Collins H (2010) Tacit and explicit knowledge. University of Chicago Press, Chicago

Doyle W (1992) Curriculum and pedagogy. In: Jackson PW (ed) Handbook of research on curriculum. Macmillan, New York

Doyle W, Rosemartin D (2012) The ecology of curriculum enactment: frame and task narratives. In: Wubbels T, den Brok P, van Tartwikj J (eds) Interpersonal relationships in education. Advances in learning environments research. Sense Publishers, Rotterdam

Eraut M (2004) Transfer of knowledge between education and workplace settings. In: Rainbird H, Fuller A, Munro A (eds) Workplace learning in context. Routledge, London

Evans K (2016) Higher vocational learning and knowledgeable practice: the newly qualified practitioner at work. In: Loo S, Jameson J (eds) Vocationalism in further and higher education: policy, programmes and pedagogy. Abingdon, Routledge

Evans K, Guile D, Harris J, Allan H (2010) Putting knowledge to work: a new approach. Nurse Educ Today 30(3):245–251

Goodwin AL, Kosnik C (2013) Quality teacher educators = quality teachers? Conceptualizing essential domains of knowledge for those who teach teachers. Teach Dev Int J Teach Prof Dev 17(3):334–346

Goodwin AL, Smith L, Souto-Manning M, Cheruvu R, Tan MY, Reed R, Taveras L (2014) What should teacher educators know and be able to do? Perspectives from practicing teacher educators. J Teach Educ. https://doi.org/10.1177/0022487114535266

Handal G (1999) Consultation using critical friends. New Dir Teach Learn 79:59–70

Kahneman D (2012) Thinking, fast and slow. Penguin Books, London

Kemmis RB, Green A (2013) Vocational education and training teachers' conceptions of their pedagogy. Int J Train Res 11(2):101–121

Koster B, Brekelmans M, Korthagen F, Wubbels T (2005) Quality requirements for teacher educators. Teach Teach Educ 21:157–176

Loo S (2007) Learning to be teachers of adult numeracy. J Educ Teach 33(4):425–440

Loo S (2012) The application of pedagogic knowledge to teaching: a conceptual framework. Int J Lifelong Educ 31(6):705–723

Loo S (2014) Placing 'knowledge' in teacher education in the English further education teaching sector: an alternative approach based on collaboration and evidence based research. Br J Educ Stud 62(3):337–354

Loo S (2018) Teachers and teaching in vocational and professional education. Routledge, Abingdon

Loo S (2020) Professional development of teacher educators in further education: pathways, knowledge, identities, and vocationalism. Routledge, Abingdon

Loughran J (2009) Is teaching a discipline? Implications for teaching and teacher education. Teach Teach Theory Pract 15(2):189–203

Loughran J, Berry A (2005) Modelling by teacher educators. Teach Teach Educ 21:193–203

Loughran J, Mitchell I, Mitchell J (2003) Attempting to document teachers' professional knowledge. Qual Stud Educ 16(6):853–873

Mayer D, Mitchell J, Santoro N, White S (2011) Teacher educators and 'accidental' careers in academe: an Australian perspective. J Educ Teach 37(3):247–260

Murray J, Male T (2005) Becoming a teacher educator: evidence from the field. Teach Teach Educ 21(2):125–142

References

Nonaka I, Takeuchi H (1995) The knowledge creating company: how Japanese companies create the dynamics of innovation. Oxford University Press, New York

Polanyi M (1966) The tacit dimension. Routledge and Kegan Paul, London

Shulman LS (1987) Knowledge and teaching: foundations of the new reform. Harv Educ Rev 57(1):1–22

Shulman LS (2005) The signature pedagogies of the professions of law, medicine, engineering, and the clergy: potential lessons for the education of teachers. In: The math science partnerships workshop: "teacher education for effective teaching and learning". National Research Council's Centre for Education, Irvine, California, US, 6–8 Feb 2005

Smeby J-C (1996) Disciplinary differences in university teaching. Stud High Educ 21:69–79

Smith K (2005) Teacher educators' expertise: what do novice teacher and teacher educators say? Teach Teach Educ 21:177–192

Swart F, de Graaff R, Onstenk J, Knezic D (2017) Teacher educators' personal practical knowledge. Teach Teach Theory Pract. https://doi.org/10.1080/13540602.2017.1368477

Swennen A, Volman M, van Essen M (2008) The development of the professional identity of two teacher educators in the context of Dutch teacher education. Eur J Teach Educ 31(2):169–184

van Oers B (1998) The fallacy of decontextualisation. Mind Cult Act 5(2):143–152

Verloop N, Van Driel J, Meijer P (2001) Teacher knowledge and the knowledge base of teaching. Int J Educ Res 35(5):441–461

Zeichner K (2007) Accumulating knowledge across self-studies in teacher education. J Teach Educ 58:36–46

Chapter 4
A Comparison of TVET Teachers and Teacher Educators' Professional Identities

Abstract This chapter uses the empirical data from the two monographs (Loo in Further education, professional and occupational pedagogy: knowledge and experiences. Routledge, Abingdon, 2019; Loo in Professional development of teacher educators in further education: pathways, knowledge, identities, and vocationalism. Routledge, Abingdon, 2020) on further education (FE) teachers, a systematic review of literature on professional identities in the further education sector and teacher educators to re-analyse the investigation of FE teachers/deliverers and teacher educators' professional identities. The findings will provide a deep thematic understanding and knowledge of these two professional identities. The themes include similarities and differences between the two educationists. Regarding similarities, the themes cover social constructions, emotional constructions, student–teacher identities, and tacit pedagogies. The differences include policies, politics and institutions; cultural factors; and modelling, research and profession under construction. Its findings offer the relevant stakeholders, such as teacher educators (from FE and compulsory education sectors), curriculum developers and managers, policymakers, and researchers, much-needed knowledge on this neglected aspect of these educationists.

Keywords Teachers · Teacher educators · Professional identities · TVET/VET · Professional · Attributes/characteristics · Pedagogy · Occupational and real-life experiences · Emotional connection · Contextual issues

Introduction

This chapter aims to ascertain the professional identities of the teachers and teacher educators in the English further education (FE) sector. Previous publications (Loo 2019, 2020) will be referred to regarding the teachers' selves, a systematic literature review of their professional identities, and the teacher educators' perspectives of themselves. There are two groups of researchers: one on teachers and the other on teacher educators' identities. Those on teachers' selves include Moore et al. (2002), Beijaard et al. (2004), and Day et al. (2007). And researchers on FE include Shain and

Gleeson (1999), Clow (2001), Viskovic and Robson (2001), Jephcote et al. (2008) and Loo (2019). Researchers that focus on teacher educators are Murray and Male (2005), Boyd and Harris (2010), and Pereira et al. (2015). And on FE educationists are Springbett (2018) and Loo (2020).

The opening chapter on the English FE characteristics and contexts would be helpful to bear in mind in reading this chapter.

The chapter structure starts with an introduction. The following section defines the contested definitions of identities (teachers and teacher educators) and reviews the relevant literature sources of the two types of educators. The third section details the related projects from the three sources. The fourth section—findings and discussion—uses the appropriate re-analysed empirical evidence and related literature sources to provide a deeper understanding of the two professional selves before concluding this study.

Relevant Literature Sources

This section focuses on the appropriate literature sources regarding the professional identities of TVET teachers (Loo 2019, Chaps. 3 and 4) and teacher educators (Loo 2020, Chap. 6). From the chapter on teachers' identities (Loo 2019), the three sources of professional knowledge were pedagogical, real life and occupational, and the three types of identities included multi, double and hybrid ones. From the chapter on teacher educators, the four themes were 'being a professional', attributes, characteristics and education, emotional connection, and contextual issues. As apparent from the findings, there are no obvious commonalities. However, an analysis of the sources behind the two professional identities will offer a deeper understanding of the possible similarities and differences starting with some definitions.

Identities are defined eclectically. Gee (2000–2001) offered four approaches to viewing identities connected to historical, institutional and sociocultural dimensions. These approaches included nature-identity that is biologically related rather than that affected by the surrounding environment. He considers this identity 'the "kind of person" I am' (Gee 2000–2001, p. 102). Gee argues that this type of identity interacts with the other three types. The second refers to institution-identity (I-Identity). He defines it as "I-Identities can be put on a continuum in terms of how actively or passively the occupant of a position fills or fulfills his or her role or duties" (Gee 2000–2001, p. 103). D-Identity or discursive identity relates to a person's trait (from genetic inheritance). Rational people view the person as an individual trait, and those interacting with the person acknowledge and accept the person. Affinity-identity (A-Identity) refers to the person's interactions with others in a group with common endeavours or practices.

For Gee, one's identity is shaped by four factors: biological, institutional, perceptions and acknowledgement by others, and interactions in a group with common interests.

Sfard and Prusak (2005) develop Gee's definition by acknowledging a person's character, nature and personality, but they argue that one's identity also includes the development of attitudes, conceptions and beliefs.

Focusing on teacher's identities, Clandinin et al. (2009, p. 141–2) relate to

> The nexus of teachers' personal practical knowledge and the landscapes, past and present, on which teachers live and work. Using a concept of 'stories to live by' is a way to speak of the stories that teachers live out in practice and tell of who they are, and are becoming, as teachers. Important to this way of thinking is an understanding of the multiplicity of each of our lives – lives composed around multiple plotlines.

Clandinin et al. (2009) focus on teacher knowledge that includes past and present ones and teaching and life experiences. This narrative approach to viewing identity provides an autobiographical perspective of identity formation.

Sharing a similar approach to the previous researchers, McKeon and Harrison (2010, p. 27) consider identities as

> The concept of 'identity' can be described as a socially and culturally constructed 'self' formed through a life's experiences and communication about these experiences. Identities should not, however, be seen as stable entities but, rather, as developing in social practice and important outcomes of participation in particular 'communities of practice' (Lave and Wenger 1991; MacLure 1993). Identity is used by individuals to justify, explain and make sense of themselves to others and to the situations in which they operate. Holland et al. (1998) stress the relationship between identity and personal history (which is brought to all situations and has a key influence on the perspectives individuals bring to the interpretation of new activities). Wenger indicates that identity can be considered as incorporating 'the past and the future in the very process of negotiating the present' (1991, p. 155), and points to the way that identity is shaped through participation in various communities of practice and that identity also shape participation in those communities.

McGregor et al. (2010) specify two types of identities for teacher educators: evolving and research ones. These identities are shaped and influenced through community interactions, like a novice teacher educator interacting with an experienced one. The other type refers to 'researcher identity', which is not necessarily the same as that of a teacher educator. For a teacher educator to be a researcher, s/he needs to re-focus and re-consider from the researcher's perspectives. Like the other researchers, they use a social constructional approach to understanding identities. However, McGregor et al. consider teacher educators as trainees of teachers and researchers.

Factors relating to biology, institutions, people's perceptions and interactions in like-minded communities shape our identities, according to Gee (2000–2001). Sfard and Prusak's (2005) identities emphasized the importance of developing one's attitudes, conceptions and beliefs. Clandinin et al. (2009) view teacher knowledge and life experiences (both past and present) as significant factors in teacher identity formation. McKeon and Harrison (2010) view identity formation within communities of practice, whereas McGregor et al. (2010) focus on community interactions as teacher educators and researchers. All the above definitions highlight the social constructions of identity formation as individuals in their agentic activities as teachers or as teacher educators operating in communities or using their biological inheritance, traits, or beliefs.

Whether a teacher or a teacher educator performs pedagogic duties individually or collectively, Lave and Wenger (1991) define professionalism as agentic practices within communities of practice and situated learning (Boyd and Harris 2010; McKeon and Harrison 2010; Williams and Ritter 2010). This learning might be informal in workplaces where novice teachers/teacher educators interact with experienced colleagues to gain full membership. These informal social interactions inform their professional identities. These identities are dynamic and fluid and are means of making sense of themselves. Lave and Wenger (1991) further emphasized that the future also informed their professional identities.

Gee (2000–2001), Sfard and Prusak (2005), Clandinin et al. (2009), McKeon and Harrison (2010), and McGregor et al. (2010) in different ways emphasized social constructions of identity-making. Jephcote and Salisbury (2009), researching FE teachers' identities, view social constructs through teachers of animal care, sociology and art. Their identities are privileged through their learners' needs (with interactions, learners' contexts and learning processes) rather than the institutional demands.

The emotional connection was identified as a theme in the teacher educators' professional identity findings. Bullough (2005) used the term community of compassion to describe the compulsory teacher educators' identities in identifying with their learners. Pereira et al. (2015) found that primary school teacher educators see their activities as a caring profession.

From FE teachers, Gleeson and James (2007) suggested that professional dispositions and practices, compliance, mediation and resistance shaped FE teachers' identities. Other factors, such as trade-offs between a professional and commitment to learners, worsening work conditions and lack of professional status, also affected their identities. Colley et al. (2007) included non-compliant with the roles and identities as teachers imposed by the FE sector, where they drew on moral and political ideas to shape their identities. These FE teachers espoused terms like conduct unbecoming and conscientious objection. Jephcote and Salisbury (2009) explained the emotional connections of FE teachers with their students despite the external pressures of the managers and policymakers. Colley et al. (2003) found tensions in FE teachers between the caring and emotional dedication to their teaching roles ('emotional comfort of belonging') and the reality of detachment to cope. Robson and Bailey (2009) researched learning support workers in the FE sector. They identified one-to-one relationships with students, and the workers' caring, adaptable, empathetic and dedication to their learners informed their identities. Loo (2019) uses emotional ecology to study the emotional connections of FE teachers regarding their pedagogic, life, and occupational experiences. He uses a conceptual framework of emotional planes and emotional knowledge to analyse these vocational teachers' relationships in their work. Zembylas's (2007, p. 357) defines emotional ecology as "emotional knowledge in a particular social and political context, including the rich connections to emotional experiences and relationships with others."

Lave and Wenger (1991) used communities of practice and situated learning to emphasize informal learning in the workplaces where the training of teachers occurred in which novices/'newcomers' in teacher education interacted with experienced/'old timers'.

Related to Lave and Wenger's concept of communities of practice are the two identity forms of newcomers (novice teachers/teacher educators) and old timers (experienced teachers/teacher educators). For Williams and Ritter (2010), collegiality, conversation, and collaboration are part of teacher educators' identity formation processes. Swennen et al. (2010) acknowledged Lave and Wenger's community of practice of teacher educators as part of a 'community of practice'; on the one hand, they also see themselves as teachers in a generic sense with a responsibility to the community. Boyd and Harris (2010) view teacher educators' identity formation differently. They used terms like 'feeling new', 'lower status', and 'supported' by those who were novice teacher educators when they entered higher education institutions as teacher educators. Even Williams and Ritter (2010) supported the findings by Boyd and Harris (2010) with fear of competing and constantly changing tensions.

Murray et al. (2011) offered three types of teacher educators' identities. The first relates to keeping their identities as ex-school teachers (featuring resistance to the higher education environment). The second is 'second-order practice' as teacher educators with its distinct pedagogy and knowledge base, referring to their previous school experiences, and the third identity refers to the pursuant of scholarship and research activities requiring time and capabilities.

Turning to FE teachers, Robson (1998) identified four professional perspectives. They refer to the control and management of learners, learning, administration, and approaches to passing on knowledge and experiences. There were other issues, such as adjustment to a teaching career and its impact on professional identity.

The above sources on the types of professional roles and their identities will offer different insights when discussing the empirical findings in the penultimate section of this chapter.

Earlier, Clandinin et al. (2009) focused on identities from the perspective of teaching knowledge and their lives (past and present). This autobiographical narrative approach implies the tacit/implicit elements of their education (as teachers and learners) and life experiences.

Pereira et al. (2015) offered five narratives of working. They are:

1. Pedagogy centres on humanistic ethics.
2. Specialists highlight the cognitive dimension of teaching.
3. The mediator focuses on the mediation between children and the social mandates governing school education.

The other two include professionals 'under construction' as researchers and academics in higher education and professionals at a critical point highlighting the challenges and difficulties of working with young learners and implementing ideas. Any of the five types of working involve tacit/implicit elements. The more obvious type is the cognitive dimension of teaching.

Robson et al. (2004) investigating FE vocational teachers' professional development offered four themes: adding value, protecting standards, sharing expertise and knowing how. The teachers viewed themselves as autonomous by giving value and going beyond the syllabus. The know-how was related to occupational and tacit forms rather than pedagogic ones. Their close interactions with their learners were significant, and they resisted the competence-based awards. The above tacit pedagogies provide a starting point for understanding teachers' and teacher educators' professional identities and development.

To date, the above literature reviews provide insights into the similarities of professional identity formation of occupational teachers and teacher educators. The remainder of this section deals with possible differences.

The first area refers to policies, politics and institutions. Springbett (2018) focused on accountability issues (e.g., Ofsted), political influences (e.g., Lingfield Report), contested quality assurance (institution), and the role of further education teaching institutions. Colley et al. (2007) studied FE teachers and their identities. Their findings suggested that these teachers drew on moral and political ideas and sought external cultures to engage with their identities. Jephcote et al. (2008) investigated FE teachers in Wales and found the intensification of their workload and the impact on their teaching. The pressures of their managers (institution) and policymakers (politics) affected their teaching towards a facilitative learning style.

Boyd and Harris (2010) identified misconceptions by (compulsory school) teacher educators working in universities of HE pedagogy (such as didactic teaching). Pereira et al. (2015) used a global neo-liberal policy background to investigate its impact on teaching institutions and teacher educators' pedagogic work.

Regarding cultures, Colley et al. (2007) identified external cultures in becoming teachers in the FE sector. Robson (1998) identified institutional cultures in FE colleges which affect the teachers' professional identities. Viskovic and Robson (2001) studied vocational teachers in New Zealand and the UK, and location and related cultures impacted the teachers' identities.

The other possible dissimilar areas include modelling, research and professionals under construction. Boyd and Harris (2010; White 2011) identified modelling good practice by teacher educators as a large part of a performative culture to show their teacher trainees. For teacher educators, modelling is a 'layered pedagogy' with two stages. The first stage refers to generic teaching strategies ad is viewed as a fundamental weakness of FE teacher training/education (Loo, 2014). The second stage relates to adapting the generic teaching approaches to a specific subject/topic, such as vocational subjects.

Research activities and identity development were studied by Boyd and Harris (2010), McKeon and Harrison (2010) and Murray et al. (2011). Boyd and Harris (2010) found that universities could offer scholarship and research activities where teacher educators in FE colleges could feel valued with access to continuing professional development. Alongside this facility might be tensions in curriculum development, a dominant activity in HE delivery. McKeon and Harrison (2010) identified the change in the identities of school teachers to teacher educators in higher education (described as 'teacher educator academic'). This transition might be challenging.

Murray et al. (2011) viewed that pursuing scholarship and research activities requires time and capabilities. Pereira et al. (2015), studying the five narratives of working for compulsory school teacher educators, identified professionals 'under construction' as both researchers and academics in universities.

This section started with definitions of identities and professionalism. It went on to critique the relevant literature sources surrounding the potential similarities and differences between the professional identities of teachers and teacher educators. The four similar areas were social construction, emotional connection, student–teacher and teacher-teacher educator identities and tacit pedagogies. The dissimilar ones were policy, politics and institutions; cultural differences; and modelling, research and professionals under construction. These areas will be used to discuss the empirical evidence in the penultimate section of this chapter.

Project Details

There are three related projects for this chapter. The first refers to the project on FE-qualified teachers with occupational experience (Loo 2019, Chap. 3), the second is from a systematic review of literature on the professional identities in the FE sector (Loo 2019, Chap. 4), and the third, professional identities of FE teacher educators (Loo 2020, Chap. 6).

The Work-Based Learning for Education Professionals Centre, Institute of Education (IOE) at University College London funded this first project. Eight volunteers, formerly trainee teachers, were on the Postgraduate Certificate of Education (Post-compulsory) programme at the IOE. A questionnaire and one-to-one semi-structured interviews were used to capture empirical evidence. The participants' taught disciplines included biology, dance, dental hygiene, health education, information technology, mathematics and radio production. Five of them were females, and three were males. The data from the two methodological approaches were transcribed (for the interviews), triangulated and analysed using the stages of generating units of meaning, classifying, etc. (Cohen et al. 2017). The project was drawn up according to the British Educational Research Association (BERA) ethical guidelines and approved by IOE.

Regarding the second project—a systematic review of literature—earlier studies by Beijaard et al. (2004), Trede et al. (2012), and van Lankveld et al. (2017) guided this project. Foster and Hammersley (1998), Petticrew and Roberts (2006), Gough (2004), and Gough et al. (2017) informed this methodological approach with the eight stages of publication gathering with a final list of 20 publications. Table 4.1 (Loo 2019, Chap. 4) was drawn up, reflecting the two research aims. They include (1) What are the characteristics of the sector's professional selves/identities? and (2) To what extent has the vocational dimension been included, and if so, in what forms? The breakdown of the methodological approaches of the 29 publications covered the theoretical and empirical, quantitative and qualitative, funding and research sites.

Eight investigators with teacher educators' experiences in FE spearheaded the third project, and the author of this chapter was also the Principal Investigation. A questionnaire, one-to-one interviews, Talking Heads (unstructured audio solo interview) and related documents formed the empirical evidence. 32 FE teacher educators participated, and IOE approved the ethics clearance based on the BERA ethical guidelines. The relevant research question for this chapter was how they viewed themselves. The empirical evidence were collated, analysed and triangulated as with the data from the first project.

Further methodological details of the three projects may be referred to in the above chapters.

Findings and Discussion

This section identifies the thematic comparisons (similarities and differences) of TVET teachers and teacher educators. Concerning similarities, the four themes are social constructions, emotional connection, student–teacher identities, and tacit pedagogies. The differences relate to policies, politics and institutions; cultural factors; and modelling, research and profession under construction.

Similarities

Social Constructions

> This ongoing iconography is a sense of therapy such as dealing with loved ones, living on my own and the impact on how I view the world. Ongoing psychological state as artist where one uses Freud's notion of dreams to feed my art and how these experiences feed into my teaching. (Teacher C)

> We never felt like parents – felt like that when I first taught and had taken a while to grow into that. Identity grows with you. One is given a label as a professional (dental hygienist) and one acts this out. I don't consider myself clever and now as a teacher, whom I consider as clever, and so I grow into it. (Teacher D)

> Being a teacher educator is a privileged position. It is a job with many hats as all teaching is. A teacher educator's role is a mid-point between the teaching profession and all the other aspects of education involving, for example, pastoral support and curriculum delivery. It is a badge between profession and wider socio-political environment [p. 1]. It is a very fragile profession and could be undermined in specifications/curriculum. We need to ask how much autonomy may, we have as educators [p. 4]. (TE25, Interview, p. 1, 4)

Findings and Discussion 65

> I think in a way being an educated teacher educator like myself should be open to all things going on in and take a more worldly view on things and not be so local and that enriches me. I find sometimes our sector is a bit of a dinosaur sometimes. However, my heart, my own experiences in initial teacher education since 2008 to 2014 has been an interesting, different and varied and a bit of a mix and I think that's been to my benefit. (TE31, Talking Head, p. 2)

McGregor et al.'s (2010) concept of identity as evolving is supported by Teachers C and D and Teacher Educators (TE) 25 and 31, but not the research dimension. This evolution of identities appeared as moving between dynamics with loved ones, independent living and the wider world and how these played out in Teacher C's work as an art teacher and his other professional experience as an architect. For Teacher C, there was also a psychoanalytical connection, exemplified by his reference to dreams and Sigmund Freud's concepts. Teacher D's identity evolution was tripartite: as a parent, professional (dental hygienist) and higher education teacher. The other two TEs (TE 25 and 31) acknowledged their identities' multi-faceted nature and connections to broader socio-political environments. Another dimension is the precarity of the communities they practised. The relevance of knowledge and life experiences delineated by Clandinin et al. (2009) is implicit in the four educators. For example, Teacher D with her knowledge and life experiences as a dental hygienist, higher education teacher and parent. With Sfard and Prusak's (2005) emphasis on developing a teacher's attitudes, conceptions and beliefs, TE31's approach was being 'open to all things', and TE25 referred to the surrounding socio-political landscape. Underpinning the four educators' pedagogic agencies were the communities they belonged to as teacher educators (TE 25 and 31) and for Teacher D, in communities as a parent, dental hygienist and teacher. These intersections between the three communities affected her sense of self (Lave and Wenger 1991; Jephcote and Salisbury 2009; McKeon and Harrison 2010).

Emotional Connections

> This ongoing iconography is a sense of therapy such as dealing with loved ones, living on my own and the impact on how I view the world. Ongoing psychological state as artist where one uses Freud's notion of dreams to feed my art and how these experiences feed into my teaching. (Teacher C)

> Teachers should undergo therapy as their pastoral roles include support of and empathy with their learners. In these two aspects, there are similarities with the roles of counsellors. (Teacher A)

> I always promote honesty to highlight my strengths and weaknesses as everybody makes mistakes and is still on a journey. The other is professional integrity as teacher educators we have a vested interest in the future of others. Another is a caring nurturing role: going the extra mile than expected but this is not in the job specification. (TE20 Interview, p. 1)

> I would never allow anything to happen to the trainees due to someone's negativity as it happened to me. I saw myself as someone who can empathize. I let the trainees know they are valued and have potential. We get the students we have; we don't blame them if something

is not going right. We have to help them to learn. Teacher trainers must help people to learn and not punish them for what they don't know. Give credit for what it is done and then give constructive feedback to develop the rest. I am the opposite of what happened to me. (TE7, Interview, p. 2)

Teachers A and C and TEs 7 and 20 subscribed to the findings of Bullough (2005), Zembylas (2007), Pereira et al. (2015) and Loo (2019). Teacher C emphasized the psychoanalytical aspect of his identity. Teacher A offered a different perspective on her emotional connections with her learners. She suggested that teachers should be aware of their strengths and weaknesses by undergoing therapy with their teacherly roles similar to counsellors'. TE20 viewed this emotional connection as part of a teacher educator's caring and nurturing role by 'going the extra mile'. TE7 learnt from his bitter experiences as a trainee teacher and used these to value his trainees as people with potential and not punish them. These different states offered broader perspectives on the emotional connections of educators.

Student–Teacher Identities

…from learner-driver to teacher practitioner to advanced teacher practitioner (Teacher A)

I've been a student and lecturer for the past ten years, so my experiences have been on both sides of the fence and in homeopathy as a student and seeing how different teachers cope. Invariably, my experiences as a teacher and as a student always apply in my teaching as I am a perpetual student. My approach to teaching is not to use a big stick and not dumb down to primary and secondary levels but work on delivery and start from the learners' world. I believe that my extensive life and work experience gained from living and working in Australia, Switzerland and the US as well as here in the UK has given me a tolerant and curiosity-focused approach to the education process. (Teacher B)

The three stages of identity formation from learner-driver to teacher practitioner and to advance teacher practitioner by Teacher A offer similarity to Lave and Wenger's (1991) newcomer and old timer regarding the stages of learning in a professional role. However, there is a more fundamental binary of student–teacher identity, which needs to be discussed in the findings by Robson (1998), Boyd and Harris (2010), Williams and Ritter (2010), Swennen et al. (2010) and Murray et al. (2011). Teacher B discussed this binary in his multi-professional experiences in homoeopathy, IT teaching and graphic design across different countries before settling in England. Connecting with this student–teacher binary identity formation are the two themes of emotional connection and social construction. He used his binary experiences to connect emotionally with his students in a supportive manner (Bullough 2005; Zembylas 2007; Pereira et al. 2015; Loo 2019). He drew from his extensive life and work experiences across the globe (social construction) to be tolerant and curious to facilitate his students' learning (Gee 2000–2001; Sfard and Prusak 2005; Clandinin et al. 2009).

Findings and Discussion 67

Tacit Pedagogies

> The transition from practice (as a dental hygienist) to teaching is easier. If I practice regularly to keep my confidence level and speed up. (Teacher D)

> It is difficult to teach manual dexterity as you need to be like a detective by being able to look into somebody's mouth, describe what you see and be able to say why it is different and work out provided they (the learners) have the theoretical knowledge and that they are able to apply it to the situation. There are transitional stages where the students can apply it to the situation. There are transitional stages where the students can apply their theoretical knowledge, each of them to detect and identify deposits on the teeth and how to remove it and having the confidence to remove them. Students are afraid to harm the patient, which it should be but experienced tutors know the amount if pressure to use and perhaps the angle of applying the instrument. That itself is quite hard to impart. (Teacher D)

> I think of myself as a member of a profession. ITE qualifications from QCF level 4 upwards are categorized as 'professional' therefore I also teach professional qualifications. This is partly shown by my qualifications and partly shown by IfL and ETF/LLUK professional standards. Teachers have a code of conduct. We are bound by the standards as set at the government level. All these things are indicators that teachers are professionals. (TE33, Interview, p. 3)

> Being a teacher educator is a privileged position. It is a job with many hats as all teaching is. A teacher educator's role is a mid-point between the teaching profession and all the other aspects of education involving, for example, pastoral support and curriculum delivery. It is a badge between profession and wider socio-political environment [p. 1]. It is a very fragile profession and could be undermined in specifications/curriculum. We need to ask how much autonomy may, we have as educators [p. 4]. (TE25, Interview, p. 1, 4)

> I enjoyed it all, and I'm now on my next stage…I think that's also what teaching is about, whatever the subject to explore, to experiment, to try. If you felt that you have failed, that's fine. It may not be for you, but you develop, and you move on. (TE31, Talking Head, p. 2)

Teacher D exhibited Pereira et al.'s (2015) 'pedagogy centres on humanistic ethics' narrative of working where she performs her teaching duties with her dental hygiene learners. These learners are in an identity transition phase, from learner to practitioner (Lave and Wenger 1991). As learners, Teacher D was aware of the learners' ethical imperative not to harm the patients. The tacit dimension concerning Teacher D highlighted the symbiotic relationship between occupational practice (as a dental hygienist) and teaching (as a dental hygiene lecturer). This symbiotic relationship offers a new dimension to Pereira et al.'s (2015) findings. Pereira et al.'s (2015) third narrative of working—as a mediator between children and the social mandates governing school education—applies to work-related/occupational education in two ways. The first relates to Teacher D as a mediator between her trainees and their course requirements concerning health and safety issues. The other way refers to the trainee hygienists as students mediating between their would-be practitioner and the eventual patients. Robson et al.'s (2004) findings reflect Teacher D's narrative regarding her wanting to add value to her learners using demonstration and simulated occupational experiences. She also seeks to protect occupational standards and share her occupational expertise with her trainees by using explicit and implicit pedagogic approaches such as simulated workshops and theoretical sessions. Teacher D's added valueness included sharing her specialist know-how tacitly with her trainees via the simulated workshops (Clandinin et al. 2009; Pereira et al. 2015). TE33 has a clear sense of professional qualifications and code to indicate her professional identity and status (Robson et al. 2004). TE25 and 31's narratives exemplified the tacit dimension regarding pastoral support, curriculum delivery, and the opportunities to explore and experiment. These themes should be evidenced in the above literature sources.

Differences

Policies, Politics and Institutions

> This is a period of massive change such as the Lingfield Report, tuition fees, organization change, and there is a feeling of being battered on all sides. So, there are lots of dilemma about teachers in FE and what is offered. My life has changed a huge amount within the last 25.5 years ago. I had a number of careers before becoming a teacher educator [worked in hotels, as a hotel catering manager, left London and moved up North, taught business in an FE college, and now a Programme Leader for the teacher training provision for my college]. I am fulfilled by my love of learning and helping others fulfill their teaching aspirations. (TE6, Talking Head, p. 1)

The above narrative by TE6 offers a different historical-socio-cultural perspective to, perhaps, a teacher in an FE institution. TE6's themes on accountability issues, political influences and the role of FE teaching institutions strongly resonate with Springbett's (2018) findings. Nevertheless, this apparent difference between teacher educators and teachers in the sector may not be somewhat divergent. Gleeson and James (2007) identified some of these issues of FE teachers relating to compliance and professional practices. Underpinning these educational changes could be viewed from a global neo-liberal policy, as Pereira et al. (2015) argued.

Cultural Factors

> Whatever I have experienced in South Africa and I have taught some tough students there, nothing has prepared me once I came into teaching in the UK. (Teacher E)

Colley et al. (2007) and Viskovic and Robson (2001) identified external cultures in becoming FE teachers. Teacher E's dual-country experiences may provide another dimension to their findings.

Findings and Discussion 69

Modelling, Research and Profession Under Construction

> You end in being in several communities: as a teacher educator in higher educational institutions (which I belong to) and slightly different from being a teacher educator in colleges. I think that the knowledge and scholarship and research route and this is a high generalization, it's only lip service in FE and there are notable exceptions (xxx College and xxx College). The grassroots network – TELL – is very helpful and there are teacher educators from colleges coming to the meetings. I think one's professional identity changes over time as one gets more confident and more knowledgeable as there is a certain degree of respect given by senior management such as asking one's opinion. (TE12, Interview, p. 3)

> It is a very fragile profession and could be undermined in specifications/curriculum. We need to ask how much autonomy may, we have as educators [p. 4]. (TE25, Interview, p. 1, 4)

> I see myself as a teacher whether I'm teaching holistic therapy, counselling or teacher training. I'm just working as a facilitator, and I'm trying to get the people there to have the best experience they can and make the most of their time. I don't really see myself as a teacher but a handholding facilitator…a companion. I have developed a humanistic counselling approach that I take with me, and stepping back, letting them do what they need to do. (TE17, Interview, p. 1–2)

> I've worked for this [FE] organization for 17 years, and in that time, I have been asked to do a lot more for a lot less. The people that suffer are the students as we have less time to read, research, to plan lessons …year on year this has got harder. Thus, we are less available for students who need more support. I don't know - after the Lingfield Report – how much value is placed on being a qualified teacher. If I said to someone that I was going to take their appendix out … I'm not trained, but I know a lot about it, they would run screaming to the hills, but it's ok to educate our young people/young citizens in this country, and any old Tom, Dick or Harry can educate them. That is fundamentally flawed, and we need to address this. As a teacher in FE, we have always been the poor relation to schools and universities, so we grapple around, we make do and mend, and I think that does nobody any favours in the long term. I think we need qualified teachers. What suddenly changes at 16 is the fact that kids come through school having failed quite profoundly in their formal education, surely there is an even greater need to have fully qualified professional people in this final 2 to 3 years … it beggar belief. Time is the biggest factor … we take a lot of work home. Last year, my average working week was 80 to 90 hours, which is unsustainable. There is a presumption that we do this in our own time, so family life suffers and ultimately our students suffer. If you're knackered and you're ratty, and you go into a classroom: they suffer, and they are the ones who pay the wages. Our resources are outdated. I use my computer, and we use our books for research. We might as well pay to come to work as we get bugger all in return. The majority of my colleagues could earn far more working in their specialist areas, and yet we still turn up every day and put our students first. It's quite funny. (TE17, Interview, p. 3)

TE 17 appeared to imply a form of modelling good practice in their pedagogic descriptions of their roles using terms like facilitator and companion (Boyd and Harris 2010; White 2011). Research activities were mentioned by TE12 in universities but appeared, at best, ad hoc in FE institutions (Boyd and Harris 2010). There were supportive networks such as TELL, which offered FE teacher educators a platform for engaging with (action) research. The precarity of teacher educators as a professional cohort was highlighted by TE25 and 17. This statement supports Pereira et al.'s (2015) professionals under construction working narrative. TE25 further delineated the specific challenges for FE teacher educators in his 17 years in the sector. The precarious professional circumstances resonate strongly with the first different theme of policies, politics and institutions (Springbett 2018). Within the different themes, there are overlaps in professional identity formation.

Conclusion

Following a literature review, this chapter intended to examine the professional identities of teachers and teacher educators in the English FE sector. Four similarities between the two educationists were identified. They were social constructions, emotional connections, student–teacher identities and tacit pedagogies. The differences between the two stakeholders included policies, politics and institutions; cultural factors; and modelling, research and profession under construction. In both the similarities and differences themes, overlaps were identified.

These findings offer stakeholders, such as policymakers, institutional managers and practitioners (both teacher educators and teachers) nuanced understanding of the two cohorts. Such insights impact the continuous professional development of the two educationist groups as activated by the institutions and stakeholders. The professional standards could be revised resulting from these findings. At the very least, a debate could arise surrounding the two types of educationists with possible (action) research spin-offs.

References

Beijaard D, Meijier PC, Verloop N (2004) Reconsidering research on teachers' professional identity. Teach Teach Educ 20:107–128

Boyd P, Harris K (2010) Becoming a university lecturer in teacher education: expert school teachers reconstructing their pedagogy and identity. Prof Dev Educ 36(1):9–24

Bullough RV Jr (2005) Being and becoming a mentor: school-based teacher educators and teacher educator identity. Teach Teach Educ 21:143–155

Clandinin DJ, Downey CA, Huber J (2009) Attending to changing landscapes: shaping the interwoven identities of teachers and teacher educators. Asia-Pac J Teach Educ 37(2):141–154

Clow R (2001) Further education teachers' constructions of professionalism. J Vocat Educ Train 53(3):407–420

Cohen L, Manion L, Morrison K (2017) Research methods in education. Routledge, Abingdon

Colley H, James D, Tedder M, Diment K (2003) Learning as becoming in vocational education and training: class, gender and the role of vocational habitus. J. Vocat Educ Train 55(4):471–498

Colley H, James D, Diment K (2007) Unbecoming teachers: towards a more dynamic notion of professional participation. J Educ Policy 22(2):173–193

Day C, Sammons P, Stobart G, Kington A, Gu Q (2007) Teachers matter: connecting lives, work and effectiveness. Open University Press, Maidenhead

Foster P, Hammersley M (1998) A review of reviews: structure and function in reviews of educational research. Br Edu Res J 24:609–628

References

Gee JP (2000–2001) Identity as an analytic lens for research in education. In: Secada WG (ed) Review of research in education, vol 25. American Educational Research Association Washington, DC, pp 99–125

Gleeson D, James D (2007) The paradox of professionalism in English further education: a TLC project perspective. Educ Rev 59(4):451–467

Gough D (2004) Systematic research synthesis. In: Thomas G, Pring R (eds) Evidence-based practice in education. Open University Press, Buckingham

Gough D, Oliver S, Thomas J (2017) An introduction to systematic reviews. SAGE Publications Ltd., London

Holland D, Cain C, Lachiotte W, Skinner D Jr (1998) Identity and agency in cultural worlds. Harvard University Press, Cambridge

Jephcote M, Salisbury J (2009) Further education teachers' accounts of their professional identities. Teach Teach Educ 25:966–972

Jephcote M, Salisbury J, Rees G (2008) Being a teacher in further education in changing times. Res Post-Compuls Educ 13(2):163–172

Lave J, Wenger E (1991) Situated learning: legitimate peripheral participation. Cambridge University Press, Cambridge

Loo S (2014) Placing 'knowledge' in teacher education in the English further education teaching sector: an alternative approach based on collaboration and evidence based research. Br J Educ Stud 62(3):337–354

Loo S (2019) Further education, professional and occupational pedagogy: knowledge and experiences. Routledge, Abingdon

Loo S (2020) Professional development of teacher educators in further education: pathways, knowledge, identities, and vocationalism. Routledge, Abingdon

MacLure M (1993) Arguing for yourself: Identity as an organising principle in teachers' jobs and lives. Br Edu Res J 19(4):311–322

McGregor D, Hooker B, Wise D, Devlin L (2010) Supporting professional learning through teacher educator enquiries: an ethnographic insight into developing understandings and changing identities. Prof Dev Educ 36(1–2):169–195

McKeon F, Harrison J (2010) Developing pedagogical practice and professional identities of beginning teacher educators. Prof Dev Educ 36(1–2):25–44

Moore A, Edwards G, Halpin D, George R (2002) Compliance, resistance and pragmatism: the (re)construction of schoolteacher identities in a period of intensive educational reform. Br Edu Res J 28(4):551–565

Murray J, Male T (2005) Becoming a teacher educator: evidence from the field. Teach Teach Educ 21(2):125–142

Murray J, Czerniawski G, Barber P (2011) Teacher educators' identities and work in England at the beginning of the second decade of the twenty-first century. J Educ Teach Int Res Pedagog 37:261–277

Pereira F, Lopes A, Marta M (2015) Being a teacher educator: professional identities and conceptions of professional education. Educ Res. https://doi.org/10.1080/00131881.2015.1078142

Petticrew M, Roberts H (2006) Systematic reviews in the social sciences: a practical guide. Blackwell, Oxford

Robson J (1998) Exploring the professional socialisation of teachers in further education: a case study. Teach Dev 2(1):43–58

Robson J, Bailey B (2009) 'Bowing from the heart': An investigation into discourses of professionalism and the work of caring for students in further education. Br Edu Res J 35(1):99–117

Robson J, Bailey B, Larkin S (2004) Adding value: investigating the discourse of professionals adopted by vocational teachers in further education colleges. J Educ Work 17:183–195

Sfard A, Prusak A (2005) Telling identities: in search of an analytic tool for investigating learning as a culturally shaped activity. Educ Res 34(4):14–22

Shain F, Gleeson D (1999) Under new management: changing conceptions of teacher professionalism and policy in the further education sector. J Educ Policy 14:445–462

Springbett O (2018) The professional identities of teacher educators in three further education colleges: an entanglement of discourse and practice. J Educ Teach 44(2):149–161

Swennen A, Jones K, Volman M (2010) Teacher educators: their identities, sub-identities and implications for professional development. Prof Dev Educ 36(1–2):131–148

Trede F, Macklin R, Bridges D (2012) Professional identity development: a review of the higher education literature. Stud High Educ 37(3):365–384

van Lankveld T, Schoonenboom J, Volman M, Croiset G, Beishuizen J (2017) Developing a teacher identity in the university context: a systematic review of the literature. High Educ Res Dev 36(2):325–342

Viskovic A, Robson J (2001) Community and identity: experiences and dilemmas of vocational teachers in post-school contexts. J in-Serv Educ 27:221–236

White E (2011) Working towards explicit modelling: experiences of a new teacher educator. Prof Dev Educ 37(4):483–497

Williams J, Ritter JK (2010) Constructing new professional identities through self-study: from teacher to teacher educator. Prof Dev Educ 36(1):77–92

Zembylas M (2007) Emotional ecology: the intersection of emotional knowledge and pedagogical content knowledge in teaching. Teach Teach Educ 23:355–367

Chapter 5
A Systematic Review of Literature of Teacher Educators' Knowledge

Abstract A systematic review of literature is a rarely employed research method in the further education (FE) sector with its distinct characteristics, including over 73.2% of the programmes (Frontier Economics in Further education workforce data for England: analysis of the 2018–19 staff individualised (SIR) data. Education & Training Foundation, London, 2020, Fig. 54) are work-related. This chapter intends to use this particular desktop research method to investigate teacher educators' knowledge. It draws on published literature covering the education sectors of FE, compulsory and higher education of teacher trainers/educators. It has two research questions in critiquing the literature sources: (1) To what extent is occupational education (vocationalism) featured? (2) What are the overlaps between the education sectors? The relevant publications are identified using previous systematic literature reviews and research methodological literature sources as guidance. A similar chapter in (Loo in Further education, professional and occupational pedagogy: knowledge and experiences. Routledge, Abingdon, 2019) using this research method was carried out relating to professional identities in the FE sector. The publications will be textually analysed concerning the research questions. The findings will enhance the understanding of this neglected group of educationists.

Keywords Teacher educators · Knowledge · Systematic review of literature · FE sector

Introduction

Teaching had been viewed as an important educational activity by the UK government as long ago as 2010 (Department for Education 2010; Department for Business, Innovation and Skills 2012). Related to this statement are teacher educators, whose job is to train prospective teachers. The aim of this chapter is to carry out a systematic review of literature on teacher educators and their know-how, which they need in training their trainees with a focus on the further education (FE) sector. Unlike the compulsory sectors (i.e., primary, and secondary), the teacher training/education in the FE sector is generic (i.e., the emphasis is on pedagogical activities and not disciplinary subjects and their related pedagogical aspects including knowledge). This difference will have implications on the findings of such a systematic review of literature. The other implication of interest for this chapter is the salient difference of programme offers in the compulsory and FE sectors. I refer to the dominant work-related offers in the FE sector (where 73.2% of its teaching staff deliver occupational/work-related programmes) (Frontier Economics 2020, Fig. 54) as opposed to those in the compulsory education sectors. As mentioned in the first chapter in this monograph, the FE sector characteristics are porosity, inclusivity, and diversity, which I argued as an amoebic space of education different to the other sectors. A lengthier delineation of the FE sector is available in Chap. 1.

Considering the salient characteristics of this sector, the research questions in carrying out a systematic review of literature, which is a specific research method, are:

1. To what extent is occupational education (vocationalism) featured?
2. What are the overlaps between the education sectors?

Regarding the book publications on teacher educators, one can ascertain three types (Loo 2020). The first group may be referred to as handbooks, which offer guidance to be teacher educators. The publications are by McEwen-Atkins and Merryfield (1996), Philpott (2014), Crawley (2016), and Czerniawski (2018). Of these, Crawley's book relates to the FE sector. The second group consists of different forms of monographs. Berry's (2008) includes the roles, professional development, abilities, and challenges of these educators in Australia. The edited book by Bates and Swennen (2012) covers contributions from over ten countries of narrative, self-study, and empirical research on topics, such as policy, practice and structures. The next book is a phenomenological study of teacher educators in the higher education sector by Davey (2013). Hadar and Brody's (2018) book focuses on institutional aspects concerning a teacher educator. Loo's (2022) edited monograph has contributions from researchers and teacher educators on teacher educators' and related stakeholders' perspectives, teacher education/training, professional identities, and professional development. The third type of teacher educators' publications are research monographs by Lunenberg, Dengerink and Korthagen (2014) on the compulsory sector in the Netherlands and Loo (2020), on the FE sector in England. The former publication is heavily researched focusing on professional roles, knowledge, and identities. It is a systematic review of literature of 137 publications. The latter research monograph by Loo (2020) delineates journeys, pathways, teaching knowledge, professional identities, and professional development.

Methodological Approach

This research method of using a systematic review of literature centres on FE teacher educators' know-how. To do this, literature sources, such as Foster and Hammersley (1998), Gough (2004), Petticrew and Roberts (2006), Boland et al. (2017) and Gough et al. (2017) provided a structure and pattern to this methodological process. This process covered the research questions formulation (as mentioned in the introduction), theoretical framework and inclusion criteria, the search for the relevant publications, and the description, evaluation, and synthesis of the chosen investigations. Below are the steps undertaken to decide on the appropriate publications:

1. The literature sources search included the following search engines: ERIC, Google Scholar, Sage, Taylor and Francis, UCL Library Services, and Web of Science. The titles searched covered teacher educators, teacher education, educator, educationists, knowledge, and know-how. These search terms came up with a maximum of 79,700 hits initially.
2. Where search facilities, such as language (English), start and end dates, and relevance, are available, these were employed. Publications included peer-reviewed academic articles (especially those from impact factored journals), chapters in edited research monographs from academic publishers, and research monographs. Excluded publications were blogs (digital and non-digital), conference proceedings, postgraduate dissertations and theses, self-publications, and think pieces articles. The rationale for this approach was to seek out academically credible publications to answer the chapter's two research questions. The duration of the publications was from 2000 to 2023. From this exercise, 3988 potentially suitable publications were identified.
3. The list of potentially relevant publications was crosschecked between two sources, such as journals and Google Scholar, to verify their academic credibility.
4. The publication titles, abstracts (where relevant) and texts of the publications were checked for their appropriateness to the aims and research questions of this study. The reference lists of the identified publications were also referred to for suitable publications for inclusion.
5. After the initial screening and after the incorporation of the search facilities, a list of 3988 was arrived at. From this list, a smaller list of 62 publications were chosen based on the research questions. From there, the final list of 52 publications was selected.
6. Table 5.1 headings in each column included (from left to right) the author, year, and title; description of the study and research aims; theoretical underpinnings; methodology; and significant findings. The word length of this table came to around 20,300 words.
7. In addition to the completed Table 5.1, the notes of the publications were used to answer the two research questions. These notes were around 25,300 words. They included additional information, such as abstracts, definitions and discussions relating to the keywords of this investigation. Pertinent information from these notes was used in the discussion section write-up.

Table 5.1 Tabular review of the characteristics of teacher educators' knowledge

Author, year and title	Description of the study	Theoretical underpinnings	Methodology	Significant findings
1. Abell et al. (2009) Preparing the Next Generation of Science Teacher Educators: A Model for Developing PCK for Teaching Science Teachers	This US-based article investigated the development of knowledge and skills in science teacher education and the opportunity to observe, practice, and reflect on the related know-how to teach science teachers. It used the pedagogical content knowledge (PCK) framework to study knowledge for doctoral students and mentors. It concluded by offering a new standard for inclusion in the ASTE: Professional Knowledge Standards for Science Teacher Educators. The article suggested that science teacher educators could use this model to prepare trainee teachers and for related doctoral preparation	It used Shulman's (1987) PCK framework for science teacher educators. Their know-how to consisted of "knowledge about curriculum, instruction, and assessment for teaching science methods courses and supervising field experiences, as well as his/her knowledge about preservice teachers and orientations to teaching science teachers" (p. 79). Relating this model to the doctoral programme (as professional development), the relevant know-how included "incoming science matter knowledge (of science and science teaching), their incoming PCK for teaching teachers, and by their opportunities and experiences in the doctoral programme" (p. 80). From the learning perspective, the article chose Lave and Wenger's (1991) community of practice for their teacher educators to develop a disciplinary knowledge base, skills for designing and enabling research, and knowledge for teaching in the subject	Instead of relying on empirical data, the article offered five vignettes (of their experiential experiences) from teacher educators. Each vignette offered specific experiential aspects. They covered instructional strategies, curriculum development, assessment, teaching learners, and orientations for teaching teachers. These experiences were then used to conceptualise a model of PCK development for science teacher educators and offer five learning trajectories	Arising from the PCK model for science teaching, five learner roles were identified in the professionalisation of science teacher educators. The first was the observer. Doctoral students could have varying pedagogic experiences at the start of the programme. So, they started by observing educators teaching teachers, and reflecting how they developed and implemented the PCK model. The second learner role related to apprentice, where he/she learned knowledge and skills and put into practice the pedagogic activities of the educators. The third learner role referred as a partner, where he/she would partner an experienced educator to design and implement a science course covering knowledge of the learners, assessments, curriculum, and instructional strategies. The fourth learner role was referred to as an independent instructor, where he/she would apply the PCK model for teaching teachers including designing, instructing, and assessing coursework. A mentor would be assigned to the independent instructor. The final role was a mentor. The duties included mentoring doctoral students to teach teachers alongside teaching formal courses, supervising apprentices, and co-teaching. The model and five learner roles provided specific directions for designing doctoral programmes for science teacher educators, and to the ASTE in its design of its professional knowledge standards for science teacher educators
2. Appova and Taylor (2019) Expert mathematics teacher educators' purposes and practices for providing prospective teachers with opportunities to develop pedagogical content knowledge in content courses	This US study centred on mathematics teacher educators' (MTEs) role in enhancing trainee teachers' pedagogical content knowledge (PCK). Emerging from this qualitative study, expert MTEs provided opportunities for teachers to develop their PCK in their mathematics content courses and develop approaches to teaching the subject	Masingila et al. (2012) found nearly all mathematics content programmes were delivered and developed by mathematics staff. The lacunae was on the teaching of these courses. MTEs were not adequately prepared to deliver these courses (Masingila et al. 2012; Sztajn et al. 2006). Sternberg and Horvath (1995) developed 'teaching expertise' as knowledge, efficiency, and teaching insight	This phenomenographical study focused on the purposes and intentions of 10 expert MTEs concerning K-8 mathematics content programmes. They interviewed the MTEs on their reflections and classroom practices with emphasis on PCK	The results indicated opportunities for trainee teachers to develop knowledge of K-8 teaching approaches in the content courses. The MTEs provided student teachers opportunities to acquire knowledge of students' understanding, such as, students' conceptions and ingenuities, misconceptions and errors, and student cognition and development. MTEs also gave their trainee teachers opportunities to develop curriculum knowledge

(continued)

Table 5.1 (continued)

Author, year and title	Description of the study	Theoretical underpinnings	Methodology	Significant findings
3. Ariza et al. (2002) Conceptions of school-based teacher educators concerning ongoing teacher education	This Spanish empirical study focused on the principles, contents, methods and evaluation of teacher education from a teacher-researcher perspective. The article suggested that ongoing teacher education needed to be developed around professional practice, curriculum innovation rather than around academic disciplines. It also identified four factors	The article began with analysing the models of teacher education. These included two divergent models: technical view of professional know-how, and a phenomenological perspective. A new conceptual model based on professional practical knowledge was put forward. The related literature sources included Porlan et al. (1998a), and Porlan and Rivero (1998). The model had seven principles. They included: (1) Knowledge based on systematic view of educational processes. (2) Social processes of ongoing teacher education. (3) Constructivist view of knowledge including theories, beliefs, interests, needs, and experiences. (4) Teacher-researcher approach to theorising a curriculum for teacher education. (5) Definition of professional knowledge as practical knowledge, e.g., practical theories, curriculum, school and professional knowledge, beliefs (students, teachers, and teacher educators), ethics, meta-disciplinary knowledge, disciplinary knowledge, socio-political knowledge, and educational disciplines knowledge. (6) Practical knowledge related to research and professional development. (7) Practical knowledge (e.g., on curriculum) based on research and ongoing evaluation	The research design centred on ongoing teacher education courses. There were 28 school-based teacher educators (21 men and 7 women). The participants were equally divided into primary and secondary schools. The curricula areas were social sciences, natural sciences and mathematics, infant and primary education, and physical education. The participants had varied teaching experiences averaging 16 years. The study used a questionnaire of inventory of beliefs focusing on principles of ongoing teacher education, professional knowledge, methods, and evaluation of ongoing teacher education. It was administered at the start and end of the courses. The quantitative data was analysed using multifactorial analytical approach	The findings related to the four themes of generic principles of ongoing teacher education, professional knowledge, methods, and evaluation of teacher education. Regarding the generic principles, the participants appeared to disagree with the technical perspective. However, they agreed with on the practical professional knowledge and reflective teacher-investigator models. Concerning professional knowledge and methods representing the technical model type, there was a split of opinions. The findings created contradictions between conception and practice. The authors explained the contradictions as "a. there coexist simultaneously in the participants explicit alternative conceptions and traditional implicit theories on teacher education; and (b) the participants have difficulty in transforming their alternative conceptions on teacher education into procedural "knowhow" and coherent "action scripts"" (p. 320)

(continued)

Table 5.1 (continued)

Author, year and title	Description of the study	Theoretical underpinnings	Methodology	Significant findings
4. Backman et al. (2019) The value of movement content knowledge in the training of Australian PE teachers: perceptions of teacher educators	This study focused on Australian physical teacher educators' (PETE) views on movement content knowledge (CK). Using Shulman's CK definition, it used interviews from nine PETEs, and the results indicated CK was perceived as physical movement performance. This conceptualisation limited the assessment value as the assessments were usually written forms and not practice-oriented ones	The study referred to Shulman's (1987, p. 8–9) CK as "the accumulation of literature and studies in content areas, and the historical and philosophical-scholarship on the nature of knowledge in those fields of study". This starting basis for thinking about teacher knowledge included pedagogical content knowledge (PCK), which he saw as the combination of content and pedagogy for teaching. Ward et al. (2015) further developed CK for PE teaching, which they called common content knowledge (CCK) that included performance (e.g., a crawl stroke) via cognitive knowledge regarding technique, tactics, rules, etc. in swimming	Seven PETE New South Wales universities in Australia took part with nine PETEs. These educators taught on physical education programmes. Data from the interviews were captured regarding CK and PCK	The findings showed the participants saw CK as "the physical performance of movement" (p. 191–192). The emphasis was on assessing the PETE student teachers' ability to teach movement. However, the assessment format was written format and not practice-based. Also, movement CK was rarely emphasised, but instead, written reflections. The reasons for it included time, academic legitimacy, ethics, and inclusion. The authors advocated a new assessment model of individual movement practices incorporating movement with optional choices and critical reflection in teaching settings
5. Banegas (2022) Teacher Educators' Fund of Knowledge for the preparation of Future Teachers	This article examined teacher educators' knowledge forms for their professional development and quality provision. The Argentinian study was based on 13 teacher educators delivering on pre-service English language education courses. The findings indicated that these educators used a range of individual and community-based funds of knowledge, culminating in a taxonomy of teacher educator fund of knowledge	Wolf (1966) propounded the term fund of knowledge to describe knowledge that was culturally developed and historically accumulated essential to one's functioning and well-being. The term included biographies (Oughton 2010), life capital and socially situated practices (Hoggs 2011) and formal and informal knowledge (Hedges 2012). Hedges (2012) provided three context-related funds of knowledge: family-based, centre-based and community-based. Hedges' classification drew on broader than disciplinary knowledge and encompassed sources and contextual settings	The study used 13 teacher educators based in Argentina with ELT experiences. The data was based on interviews and significant circles (Esteban-Guitart 2016) using circles to identify participants' funds of identity	The findings of these teacher educators' funds of knowledge included self-efficacy, disciplinary knowledge (language content), situated practices, and beliefs. A taxonomy consisted of two knowledge types (knowledge of ELT and language teacher education pedagogy) with sub-types and funds of knowledge (individual and community-based)

(continued)

Methodological Approach   79

Table 5.1 (continued)

Author, year and title	Description of the study	Theoretical underpinnings	Methodology	Significant findings
6. Berry (2007) Reconceptualizing Teacher Educator Knowledge as Tensions: Exploring tension between valuing and reconstructing experiences	This empirical investigation by a teacher educator of 28 trainee teachers at Monash University, Australia, focused on her knowledge development as tensions. The study enhanced her understanding of practice and added to her professional knowledge as a teacher educator	Bullough (1997) used autobiographical stories to analyse critical incidents (Measor 1985). The tensions identified by Berry (2005) included telling and growth, confidence and uncertainty, action and intent, safety and challenges, valuing and reconstructing experience, and planning and being responsive (p. 120)	Data collected from 28 trainee teachers from the Australian university in the teacher educator's biology classes ranged from autobiographical accounts to email correspondence with a student teacher (also refer to Berry (2009) (No. 7))	The findings surrounding tensions and the author's practice enabled a reframing conventional notions of knowledge development and construction of teaching about teaching using ongoing analysis of one's personal experiences. The results were reflected in Berry (2009)
7. Berry (2009) Professional self-understanding as expertise in teaching about teaching	This publication was a teacher educator's self-study in Australia regarding knowledge of teaching about teaching	The related literature sources included complexity, and issues of teaching as a teacher educator, required expertise, and self-awareness and understanding. Teacher educator's preparation had lamentable research attention (Ducharme 1996; Korthagen et al. 2001; Zeichner 2005). Teacher educator's knowledge was complex (Berry 2004) due partly to its characteristic—teaching about teaching (Loughran 2007). Korthagen et al. (2005) identified two viewpoints of teacher educator expertise—'big picture' relating to know-how and specific expertise in contextual settings as a complex dual role. Its complexity includes its tacit practice knowledge (Clandinin 1986; Eraut 1994; Loughran 2007), which needs explicating (Smith 2005) to trainee teachers. Teacher educators require to have self-knowledge (i.e., knowledge of one's know-how and skills (Eraut 1994)) and self-awareness (i.e., ability to reflect and assess one's behaviour and actions) (p. 309). For Kelchtermans (2005), self-understanding forms part of his personal interpretive framework. The framework is dynamic and biographical and viewed as process (of self-construction) and product. Thus, self-study is a tool to study self-understanding (Hamilton and Pinnegar 1998)	This self-study used data from the participant's sources. They included autobiographical accounts, video of teaching sessions, journal, field notes, colleague's observation of the classes, student assignments, interviews with trainee teachers and email correspondence with one student teacher	Tensions were identified in this self-study relating to telling trainee teachers about teaching and offering opportunities for them to learn about teaching for themselves, teacher educators having the confidence to investigate uncertain teaching approaches in teacher education, discrepancies between achieving aims and undermined by their actions, facilitating trainee teachers in challenging pedagogic approaches and going beyond these approaches, and getting trainees to value their personal experiences and going beyond the experiences. The author argued these tensions in developing her knowledge of practice as a teacher educator needed specific qualities, such as sensitivity, ability to identify different learning opportunities, trust in oneself and students, risk taking, modelling one's practice and capability to share intellectual control

(continued)

Table 5.1 (continued)

Author, year and title	Description of the study	Theoretical underpinnings	Methodology	Significant findings
8. Berry and Forgasz (2018) Disseminating Secret-Story-Knowledge through the Self-Study of Teacher Education Practices	The two researchers focused on secret-story-knowledge using self-study methodology by teacher educators. Its foci were on pedagogy development and their professional knowledge -secret-story-knowledge. This Australian study redefined the work by teacher educators	The researchers drew on Clandinin and Connelly's (1995) landscape metaphor regarding teacher professional knowledge in the classroom with students and in professional places with others. Mining the former knowledge type, they investigated the sacred stories, i.e., "the official stories of teacher professional knowledge espoused in public policy and theory" (p. 237)	This project used self-study as a methodological approach (Hamilton and Pinnegar 1998). The two teacher educators, as participants, aimed to understand, highlight, and value in their role as teacher educators and control their professional activity and status	From their reflection, they argued teacher education should not be understood only as technical application of knowledge to practice but should include narratives concerning contextualised, relational, and moral dimensions. These stories were part of their professional knowing (and professional resistance)
9. Berry and Scheele (2007) Professional Learning Together: Building Teacher Educator Knowledge Through Collaborative Research	This empirically based chapter contribution focused on understanding and managing 'telling and growth' (Berry 2004) tension by teacher educators in teaching and learning about teaching. The tension between 'telling and growth' arises out of the teacher educators' competing needs to 'tell' prospective teachers what they need to know about teaching while also acknowledging the important task of helping prospective teachers to 'grow', through providing experiences for learning about teaching for themselves" (p. 192)	There were: teacher educators who adopted the 'telling and showing' approach (Myers 2002, p. 131) where knowledge regarding teaching was driven by using stories, ideas, and concepts to trainee teachers. However, the authors argued that this banking model of education (Freire 1970) was not helpful for trainee teachers (Korthagen 2001). A consequence was that transmissive approaches were used in teacher education. But the teacher educators who resisted this technical-rational approach had issues regarding identity constructions, and development of knowledge concerning their roles. Thus, this chapter centred on the 'telling and growth' research approach to understanding teaching and learning about teaching	The data was conducted over an academic year within Biology methods of 25 students in Australia. Sam, a teacher educator colleague, acted as a participant-observer by discussing with prospective teachers about their learning. Sam supported her colleague, Amanda, in interpreting, questioning and clarifying the biology methods sessions. Also, this methodological approach enabled Sam's research involvement provided her own pedagogical experience as a beginning teacher educator. Data gathered included Sam's observations in the biology methods sessions, written journals from Sam and Amanda, and pre-sessional briefings between the two researchers. The students' comments were anonymised	The findings were presented in three ways: (1) Amanda's learning about teaching—intentions, enactment, and interpretation; (2) Sam's learning about practice—experiences, relationships, and reflection; and (3) Sam and Amanda's collaborative approach to researching practice The overviews of this self-study included the potential to explore and articulate their professional identities and facilitate knowledge growth regarding their practices. A self-study approach provided a "bridge between what can be learnt by individual teacher educators and how an understanding of the work of individuals can contribute more broadly to the development of the knowledge of the profession of teacher education" (p. 204)

(continued)

Methodological Approach   81

Table 5.1 (continued)

Author, year and title	Description of the study	Theoretical underpinnings	Methodology	Significant findings
10. Beswick and Goos (2018) Mathematics teacher educator knowledge: What do we know and where to from here?	The article by two journal editors of the Journal of Mathematics Teacher Education focused on mathematics teacher educator (MTE) knowledge. This review of two articles discussed teacher knowledge conceptualisations covering teacher educators' characteristics and examining contemporary developments		This article reviewed articles published in a special issue	Leikin et al. (2018) (Israeli study) developed Jaworski's (2002) teaching triad model—Challenging Content for Mathematics Teachers—regarding mathematics teacher educators' role in teacher education/training. Masingila et al. (2018) focused on MTEs knowledge. For Masingila et al. (US study) (2018), their focus was mathematical knowledge for teaching (MKT) referred to MTEs content knowledge in helping elementary preservice teachers to learn
11. Blankman et al. (2015) Primary teacher educators' perceptions of desired and achieved pedagogical content knowledge in geography education in primary teacher training	This Dutch project studied primary school teacher educators' perceptions of pedagogical content knowledge (PCK) in geography education. Thirty-nine teacher educators participated in a questionnaire. The findings included the participants did not view their trainee students as having significant knowledge about geography. However, they suggested that their trainees had syntactic knowledge and beliefs regarding the discipline. The teacher educators suggested more teaching and emphasis on subject knowledge to increase their knowledge	The literature review section focused on Shulman's (1986) PCK within his seven knowledge bases typology. PCK was a contested terrain (Van Driel et al. 1998; Cochran et al. 1991) and argued for a more integrated concept. Others (e.g., Turner-Bisset (1999)) advocated the difficulty in distinguishing content knowledge and PCK. Martin (2005) developed three forms of content knowledge by asking what, how and why in applying content knowledge. This framework was adopted by the International Charter on Geographic Education of the International Geographical Union. For the researchers, they viewed three levels of geography teaching: teacher educator, trainee teacher, and student	This study posed three research questions on the desired and achieved levels of PCK-G for primary student teachers, and related factors of the desired PCK-G level in initial teacher education in primary education. A questionnaire was administered to 39 teacher educators from the primary teacher-training network of the Royal Dutch Geographical Society. The 62 questions focused on their perceptions of PCK-G, content knowledge, syntactic knowledge, and beliefs. Quantitative measurements (e.g., means and standard deviations) were applied to ascertain the results	The results included the primary teacher educators believed that PCK-G was necessary. However, there were differences regarding the achieved level of PCK-G. Content/subject knowledge was not present in the students' know-how (e.g., topographic names and spatial issues explanation). The participants felt that there should be a higher level of substantial knowledge, as a prerequisite for syntactic knowledge

(continued)

Table 5.1 (continued)

Author, year and title	Description of the study	Theoretical underpinnings	Methodology	Significant findings
12. Bourke et al. (2023) Teacher educators' knowledge about diversity: what enables and constrains their teaching decisions?	This Australian study focused on university teacher educators' perspectives of knowledge regarding diversity and its impact on teaching. The findings uncovered eleven discourses, and the researchers provided three factors for preparing preservice teachers	The literature review section focused on three aspects: teacher educators' knowledge base, diversity, and reflectivity. Teacher educators' knowledge and diversity teaching (Dunac and Demire 2017; Jovanovic et al. 2014; Rowan et al. 2021) centred on population heterogeneity and its impact on educational access and outcomes. Knowledge of diversity (Adams et al. 2016; Cobb 2018) provided a theoretical grounding for this project. Archer's (2007) social theory of reflectivity considered how knowledge was enacted in pedagogic practice and normalised through discourse	Participants included 32 Australian and New Zealand teacher educators from nineteen universities. Their academic roles included lecturers, professors, and deans with experiences of initial teacher education courses. Data was captured via two social labs where activities including dialogue, listening and ideas exchange occurred. These audio recordings were transcribed along with group notes. The project aims included the participants' perspectives of knowledge and diversity and the related factors enabling and constraining teaching in their universities	The findings covered personal emergent properties (PEPs) knowledge (e.g., personal, structural, and cultural). There were sub-categories of discourses of the three PEPs knowledge. With personal PEPs, the discourses included knowledge as experience, diversity as inclusion, and social justice ideals. With structural PEPs, the discourses ranged from siloed knowledge, tokenism, uncertainty, time scarcity (leading to work intensification), and catalytic property of professional standards. Regarding cultural PEPs, the discourses were deficit discourse of students' mindsets, and occupational culture
13. Brown et al. (2016) Sliding subject positions: knowledge and teacher educators	This article part of a broader study by English researchers focused on teacher educators and subject knowledge. Specifically, this study centred on teacher educators' shifting subject knowledge identities and identities due to structural changes (via the School Direct model from 2012). It used a Lacanian model of subjectivity to investigate how teacher educators and their trainee teachers re-imagined their selves due to market-led teaching environments	This school-based project highlighted how subject knowledge was conceptualised in pre-service teacher education due to structural changes in the National Curriculum core areas, resulting in a reduction of trainee recruitment numbers in some subject areas (e.g., music, drama, and art). The consequence of the change impacted teacher educators and their trainees regarding subject knowledge and identity. Lacan's (1986, 2007, 2008) model of subjectivity was used to understand these changes. Subject knowledge was susceptible to changes to curriculum and training arrangements (Price and Willet 2006). Structural changes on school practices (e.g., assessment, prescriptive curriculum, and school inspection) created a culture of performativity that impacted teacher education (also roles and identities of teacher educators and trainee teachers) (Brown and England 2004; Askew et al. 2010; Pampaka et al. 2012)	The article used data from a study of teacher educators from compulsory school experiences. Data from interviews centred on teaching staff of teacher educators, managers, mentors and trainee teachers and their perspectives of subject knowledge with practice. The researchers provided three case studies to show impact of teacher educators' identities with minority curriculum subjects and reduction of subject knowledge in some university programmes	The findings used three teacher educator case studies to explain changes to subject knowledge and reconfiguration of educators' embodiment of subject knowledge. In the social sciences (e.g., sociology and psychology), one university teacher educator described how this subject area was condensed/reduced to a generic form to provide a broader coverage of several disciplines. This commodification of teacher education resulted from funding residing with the trainees and, ultimately, to the school via the School Direct model. The second case study involved the university's art department. Due to the reduction in trainees in this discipline (and its status), a four-staff team became one. This structural rearrangement affected the educator's ability to provide adequately theoretical input to the Arts trainee teachers. As a result, the more practice-oriented School Direct model reduced the trainees' exposure to the depth and breadth of the subject knowledge. The final case study centred on a teacher educator managing over a hundred trainees indicated the marginalisation of subject knowledge in favour of aligning teaching schemes. These schemes included the school's preferred practice approach. This practice led to a commodification of the university's theoretical input of subject knowledge using market metaphors. The university's role by its teacher educators became a mentoring one

(continued)

Table 5.1 (continued)

Author, year and title	Description of the study	Theoretical underpinnings	Methodology	Significant findings
14. Bullock (2009a, b) Becoming a Teacher Educator: The Self as a Basis-for-Knowing	This publication was a self-study of a teacher educator in Canada, where 'self' was perceived as a basis-for-knowing	Self-study refers to making tacit aspects of teacher education practices explicit for related stakeholders (e.g., trainee teachers, practicing teachers and teacher educators) (Loughran 2004). Bullock's self-study accorded him to rely on his professional knowledge, interrogate assumptions and develop principles based on his teacher education experiences	Using self-study as a research methodological process (Loughran 2004), Bullock examined the role of story/narrative in his self-study project. It included naming prior assumptions explicitly. Relevant to this narrative included 'secret, sacred and cover stories' (Connelly and Clandinin 1995) to understanding teachers' professional knowledge	In Bullock's self-study, he referred to his learning from teacher education delivery and knowing-in-action. With the first aspect, he acknowledged the tensions between perceiving teachers' professional knowledge as propositional (Shulman 1987) and experiential (Connelly and Clandinin 1995). Bullock saw self-study as a methodological approach to providing a 'basis-for-knowing' and not a knowledge base for teacher education, where narratives/stories played a crucial part in transforming a teacher educator
15. Bullock (2009a, b) Learning to think like a teacher educator: making the substantive syntactic structures of teaching explicit through self-study	This article approached the study of teacher educators from the basis of 'knowing' and not a knowledge base. It used self-studies as empirical data. The argument related to the construction of a pedagogy of teacher education went beyond transmitting best classroom practices to trainees. It required a sustained, systematic, and careful inquiry into one's practice through self-study. In this regard, teaching was a discipline	The author used supporting literature sources (e.g., Bullough and Pinnegar 2001; Loughran, Hamilton, LaBoskey and Russell 2004; Kitchen 2005; Berry 2007; Bullough 2007; Ritter 2007; Zeichner 2007) of self-study to investigate his teacher education practice	This Canadian article used the self-study of the author during the three years of doctoral (Ph.D.) studies and as a beginning teacher educator. The autobiographical elements of this approach included reflection-in-action experiences as a teacher educator, past experiences as a teacher candidate, and experiences created with teacher candidates (p. 294)	The findings related to the three types of learning. Reflection-in-action—this approach is related to the reframing of experiences that happen in decision-making or action-taking. Syntactic teaching structures, i.e., actions of teaching, were known to those who had been to school. However, the substantive structure of teaching was elusive as it is related to specific teaching contexts using perceptual knowledge (i.e., 'phronesis' Korthagen and Kessels (1999)). Three points resulted from this study: to become a teacher educator required careful analysis of teaching and learning experiences to construct knowledge, identify and re-interrupt own experiences as a teacher candidate, and create and sustain a context of productive learning (p. 302)

(continued)

Table 5.1 (continued)

Author, year and title	Description of the study	Theoretical underpinnings	Methodology	Significant findings
16. Carpendale et al. (2020) Modelling Meaningful Chemistry Teacher Education Online: Reflections from Chemistry Preservice Teacher Educators in Australia	This Australian study focused on three chemistry teacher educators from universities in the state of Victoria. Its aim was to examine the online delivery of preservice teacher education classes from the technological pedagogical content knowledge (TPACK) perspective. The thematic reflections provided illustrations of the educators' applications of digital technologies to support their trainee teachers' learning in chemistry education	The COVID-19 global pandemic necessitated a dramatic shift from face-to-face to online delivery (Ottenbreit-Leftwich et al. 2010; Uerz et al. 2018). Others (e.g. Brantley-Dias et al. 2013) separated technology integration from technology-enabled learning. Teacher educators might facilitate preservice teachers' learning experiences by modelling teaching approaches for delivering chemistry using digital technologies (Brantley-Dias et al. 2013). This activity could contribute to the teachers' development of TPACK (Shulman 1987)	Teacher education courses from Monash University, Deakin University and the University of Melbourne participated in the study. The article provided contextual documents (e.g., curriculum and assessments) and universities contexts. The three Chemistry teacher educators offered reflective vignettes based on a semester impacted by COVID-19 pandemic in the country	From the vignettes, four themes emerged. They were (1) reframing challenges as opportunities, (2) purposeful decision-making in online practices, (3) modelling TPACK for delivering chemistry, and (4) interplay of university-practicum. The results provided four recommendations. These covered avoidance of 'Zoom fatigue' in an online session, explicit mention by teacher educators to their trainee teachers the pedagogical decisions underpinning their teaching approaches, incorporating of more microteaching experiences to overcome lack of classroom teaching experiences, and significance of developing trainee teachers' digital competencies
17. Castera et al. (2019) Self-reported TPACK of teacher educators across six countries in Asia and Europe	This empirically based study of teacher educators' technological pedagogical and content knowledge (TPACK) model of the seven factors. The project findings included: a relative stability of the model framework in the six countries in Asia and Europe, the relative differences of university educators' TPACK perspectives in the countries, the age dependency and TPACK factors, and an independence of gender/academic level and the model	The TPACK model by Mishra and Koehler (2006) was used to study teacher educators' integration of technology in classrooms. The framework included technological knowledge or Shulman's (1987) pedagogical knowledge and content knowledge. Its application covered selection and application of hardware and software that were pedagogically appropriate and effective (Voogt and McKenney 2017) The seven factors in the model were: technological knowledge (TK), pedagogical knowledge (PK), content knowledge (CK), technological content knowledge (TCK), technological pedagogical knowledge (TPK), pedagogical content knowledge (PCK), and technological pedagogical content knowledge (TPCK)	The research questions included: (1) Are university teachers' perceptions of technological, pedagogical, and content knowledge in the six countries compatible with the TPACK model? (2) To what extent are these factors related to university teachers' demographic factors (i.e., gender, age, and level of academic degree)? The questionnaire sample included 574 university teacher educators (offering teacher education programmes) from eight institutions in six countries. The survey was carried out in two languages: English and French. The six countries were Bhutan, Denmark, Estonia, France, Malaysia, and Pakistan	The quantitative findings were: (1) Project supported the seven-factor model across the six countries, (2) Differences of university educators' TPACK perceptions were found in the Bhutanese sample (e.g., low professional esteem), with few differences in PCK (higher score in France than Estonia and Pakistan), and in TPK (higher score in Pakistan than France implying a low technological integration in the classrooms), (3) Clear relationship between age and perceptions of TPACK but not statistically found (perhaps, due to small sample sizes and the issue of multiple comparisons), and (4) No gender and level of initial training from the TPACK factors

(continued)

Methodological Approach 85

Table 5.1 (continued)

Author, year and title	Description of the study	Theoretical underpinnings	Methodology	Significant findings
18. Ceallaigh (2022) Designing, navigating and nurturing virtual learning spaces: Teacher educators' professional development priorities and potential pathways	This investigation from Ireland focused on teacher educators' (with teaching experiences in compulsory education sectors) discipline-specific knowledge base and pedagogical competences for online learning environment. It used survey, interviews and focus group interviews to gather empirical data. The findings highlighted challenges in conceptualising contemporary pedagogy, implementing teaching process, and facilitating student interactivity. The author suggested the findings also provided ideas for professional development for teacher education	The review section discussed the increase of online education and the necessary competences. Researchers (e.g. Garrison and Kanuka 2004; Huang 2019; Abrami et al. 2011). attested to the growth of online and blended educational provisions, and deeper understanding of these pedagogic approaches were required. In developing a relevant knowledge base, the authors drew on collective activities (Seifert and Ban-Tal 2021). Garrison et al.'s (2000) theoretical framework used three interdependent constructions—teaching presence, social presence and cognitive presence—to offer a collaborative framework	The project used an online questionnaire (for 123 teacher educators), eight semi-structured interviews and one focus group interview to gather data. Systematic coding and thematic analysis were applied	The themes from the analysis were: (1) curating and crafting contemporary pedagogy, (2) implementing instructional process, (3) cultivating learner interactivity and discourse, and (4) catalysts for transformation. Significant challenges to these thematic activities were highlighted. The participants reported a lack of confidence and competence to the technological and pedagogical skills to deliver asynchronous programmes. There were also issues regarding deconstructing and reconfiguring their professional identities and struggling to ensure success of their prospective teachers. The teacher educators found it difficult to foster authentic student engagement with the realities of teaching and learning alongside a lack of discipline-specific pedagogies. However, characteristics of their pedagogic experiences positively affected their knowledge understanding. They valued the collaborative nature of this exercise
19. Chauvot (2008) Curricula Knowledge and the Work of Mathematics Teacher Educators	This US article focused on mathematics teacher educator curricular knowledge, i.e., the context of mathematics education for the mathematics teacher educator. This study built on previous self-study that examined knowledge growth and structure of a novice mathematics teacher educator using Shulman's (1986) subject matter content knowledge, pedagogical content knowledge and curricular knowledge	The study used Shulman's (1986) definition of curricular knowledge (CK). CK included knowledge of different courses and materials for teaching; indications and contradictions, lateral curricular knowledge (in other subjects); and vertical curricular knowledge (different levels of the same subject knowledge)	It used three hypothetical cases to illustrate curricular knowledge in varying contexts. The first one related to a university-based educator of an undergraduate secondary mathematics methods programme. The second case highlighted a secondary school curriculum supervisor who provided professional development for mathematics teachers. The third example showed a university-based faculty member who mentored mathematics education doctoral students	The findings centred on the three hypothetical case studies and the four aspects of CK. They included collaboration and reflective analysis are important aspects of teacher educators' professional development. Knowledge was developed via communities of practice (Zaslavski et al. 2004). By adopting the notion of layers (of doctoral candidates, practicing teachers, trainee teachers, and young/child learners), researchers could further study the work of teacher educators. It argued that this study provided an understanding of curricular knowledge construction and the work of mathematics teacher educators

(continued)

Table 5.1 (continued)

Author, year and title	Description of the study	Theoretical underpinnings	Methodology	Significant findings
20. Chick and Beswick (2018) Teaching teachers to teach Boris: a framework for mathematics teacher educator pedagogical content knowledge	The aim of this article was to provide a framework for the pedagogical content knowledge (PCK) of mathematics teacher educators (MTEs) in developing pre-service teachers' (PSTs) PCK for mathematics teaching/delivery. The framework built on PCK research and categorised the work of teacher education	The authors used a school mathematics teaching pedagogical content knowledge (SMTPCK) framework by Chick and Beswick (2013) where it used a set of filters to study PCK for teaching school mathematics to identify teachers' work. This framework was then adapted for mathematics teacher educators (hence, MTEPCK). This adapted framework also included school students and their beliefs (knowledge of content and students) (Ball et al. 2008)	This Australian case study centred on the first author's teaching experiences of secondary school PSTs on a module, which lasted 9 weeks. The data included online discussion posts. Activities included aspects of mathematics teaching, such as mathematics teacher educators' know-how. The focus of this analysis was to ascertain if the MTEPCK framework was useful for identifying MTE knowledge and categorising knowledge types	The results showed that around two-thirds of the categories in the framework (Table 1) were evidenced. There were instances where the MTE acted as a mathematics content teacher the know-how was drawn from the SMTPCK model highlighted the complexity of the work The authors suggested that the intuitive actions built explicit knowledge by providing evidence. Lastly, the MTEPCK framework offered an exhaustive and static body of know-how, but the know-how of an effective mathematics teacher educator should be dynamic, evolving, and subject to scrutiny
21. Cooper (2013) Using Critical Experiences to Build Understanding of Science Teacher Educators' Pedagogical Knowledge	This study focused on science teacher educators' (STEs) professional development of pedagogical knowledge (PK) using critical experiences (CEs). The findings revealed the importance of individuals' themes, and their dispositions shaped their beliefs and attitudes in developing PK	The literature review featured pedagogy, PK, and CEs. With pedagogy, the study relied on personal (internal) (also known as PK) and professional (external) connections in considering dispositions (i.e., action based on beliefs) (Katz and Raths 1985). References of PK included Shulman's (1987) typology of teacher knowledge, particularly PK. Morine-Dershimer and Kent's (1999) PK model was used to provide an interpretive approach to understanding a teacher's beliefs/perceptions and personal practical experiences with reference to STEs. Sikes et al.'s (1985) CEs definition was employed for this study to capture a teacher's PK	The study had three research questions relating to CEs' role in developing PK for STEs, the participants' PK concepts over their careers, and the precursors to developing PK The eight participants were STEs from six Australian universities and formerly secondary school science teachers. They academic positions ranged from early to mid and late careers. Data was gathered from interviews, and in the analysis, CEs featured throughout their careers, starting from secondary school teaching	The findings showed that the participants' CEs were personal experiences that evoked relatable emotions and learnt from these incidents. CEs also allowed the participants to study a person's thinking and teaching practice. The STEs PK concepts changed over their careers. Reflection and risk-taking with teaching practice added to the complexities of PK

(continued)

Methodological Approach

Table 5.1 (continued)

Author, year and title	Description of the study	Theoretical underpinnings	Methodology	Significant findings
22. Demoiny (2018) Social studies teacher educators who do race work: A racial-pedagogical-content-knowledge analysis	This US study centred on 11 teacher educators delivering race topic in social studies methods programmes. It used racial-pedagogical-content-knowledge (RPCK) framework to analyse the empirical data. The data was based on semi-structured interviews and documents. The findings provided approaches of incorporating race into the courses using the RPCK framework	This project used critical race theory (CRT) and RPCK frameworks. CRT (Delago and Stefanic 2001; Ladson-Billings and Tate 1995) theoretical and methodological approaches were used in this study, where racism was normalised and embedded in society. The authors recognised the varied identities of individuals relating to gender, sexual orientation, and socioeconomic status RPCK framework referred to Shulman's (1987) typology of teacher knowledge with special reference to pedagogical content knowledge. Chandler (2015) developed Shulman's PCK for race work in social studies to become RPCK. Chandler and Hawley (2017, p. 5) defined the framework as "a construct that melds content knowledge, pedagogical content knowledge and a working racial knowledge through the application of CRT"	The research question of this investigation was on the approaches that the teacher educators apply RPCK framework in their teaching courses. 11 social studies teacher educators (SSTEs) from Carnegie classified universities in US participated in this project due to their conference presentations and journal articles publications. Qualitative data capture included semi-structured interviews and documents (e.g., university department mission statements and course information). The analytical processes included coding and categorisation	The findings indicated the participants believed race was integral to understanding the social studies disciplines with RPCK (i.e., content knowledge, pedagogical content knowledge and a working racial knowledge) The study showed RPCK could be used in social studies courses and offered language consistency in teaching. The authors also argued that study of white supremacy should be included in the RPCK framework to provide a comprehensive approach

(continued)

Table 5.1 (continued)

Author, year and title	Description of the study	Theoretical underpinnings	Methodology	Significant findings
23. Duch and Nielsen (2022) Stakeholder Perspectives on Vocational Teacher Education and Teacher Educators Roles in Supporting Coherence	This research monograph chapter focused on how teacher educators in Denmark balance the different perspectives and support a sense of coherence among vocational schoolteachers. It used a range of qualitative studies to examine how teacher educators support a coherent education for vocational teachers. This study covered policy analysis for 2014–2017 and 2019–2021. The findings uncovered the political interests regarding teacher educators' practices to facilitate appropriate training of vocational teachers at level 6 (of the European Qualifications Framework). This chapter examined the different expectations of vocational teachers and managers of the institutions for 2014–2017. The findings from three vocational schools covered stakeholders' expectations. These included interest from the policy level in how teacher educators' practice influenced the space for action and conflicted interests between vocational teachers and managers	The literature review consisted of three parts. The first part was related to vocational teachers and teacher education. The next aspect was coherence and its application to teacher education, and finally, the approach of teacher educators to the roles. Regarding the first part, the Danish Ministry of Education emphasised the connection between theory and practice in the Diploma of Vocational Pedagogy programme. Other factors included technological developments (Andersson and Köpsén 2015), curriculum and identity (Avis and Bathmaker 2006) and adult learning (Illeris 2003). The concept of coherence in teacher education is classified into conceptual and structural coherence. The former refers to visions, ideas and values (Hammerness 2006; Tatoo 1996), and the latter relates to practical training and progression (Hammerness 2006). Additionally, there are two types of coherence, such as biographical and transitional (Heggen and Smeby 2012). Policies tend to relate to structural coherence. For Lund (2018), teacher educators have a double pedagogical perspective that addresses the teacher education, the teaching practice for trainee teachers, and the relationship between the two points	The two research questions are: How do teacher educators support coherence in a teacher education programme for vocational teachers? What challenges and tensions be condensed across research studies focussing on stakeholder perspectives? The project re-analysed data from three published qualitative studies by the chapter authors. One relates policy analysis to documents and interviews. The second study refers to two studies of five vocational colleges using focus group interviews, interviews and observations for 2014–2017 and 2019-2021. These projects covered the expectations of vocational teachers and managers from the teaching institutions. The final project investigated teacher educators' experiences and findings from their research and development activities	The findings sections were thematically structured. The first referred to coherence in policy-framing teacher educators' space for action. From 2010 to 2018, there appeared "to be a lack of interest in more theoretical perspectives in education, the ability to reflect on a profession as a teacher and the perspectives of lifelong learning" for the trainee teachers (p. 69). The second theme was concerned with coherence at the vocational schools from the trainee teachers' and managers' perspectives. Trainee teachers' coherence depended on collaborative opportunities. They focused on biographical coherence and transitional coherence. The managers focused on conceptual coherence, structured coherence, and programme–fieldwork coherence. The teacher educators needed to factor in these types of coherences in their teacher education programmes. For these teacher educators, the different coherences provided tensions and challenges in their pedagogic roles. The final theme centred on the tensions arising from the use of different knowledge in projects and findings. These affected the teacher educators' sense of coherence. The chapter authors used knotworking (Engeström 2001) as a concept (i.e., how different perspectives were presented, analysed, and discussed) to discuss this phenomenon. The findings indicated that these educators were willing to share the project results for analysis

(continued)

Methodological Approach 89

Table 5.1 (continued)

Author, year and title	Description of the study	Theoretical underpinnings	Methodology	Significant findings
24. Faikhamta and Clarke (2013) A Self-Study of a Thai Teacher Educator Developing a Better Understanding of PCK for Teaching about Teaching Science	This article was based on a self-study of a Thai teacher educator about pedagogical content knowledge (PCK) for teaching science student teachers and its engagement of field-based science methods course in the trainee teachers' development of their PCK. It used qualitative data. The findings suggested this study facilitated develop trainee teachers' PCK. Also, it enhanced teacher educators' PCK for science teaching and curriculum development	Shulman's (1987) concept of PCK was the starting basis in this article's literature review where he argued pedagogy needed to blend with content PCK might be typologised as general (where concepts and strategies were specific to disciplines), domain (that related to curricula studies of chemistry or biology within the sciences with specific concepts and technical terms of each study) (Geddis 1993; Veal and MaKinster 1999). PCK from teacher educators' perspective, it meant understanding trainee teachers' knowledge about teaching and learning science; knowing strategies for facilitating their trainee teachers' learning; assessing and evaluating their learners-teachers' learning; and planning educators' teaching practices in developing teachers' PCK	This phenomenological self-study methodological approach used qualitative data from videoed classroom teaching, journal entries, student teachers' journals and assignments, students' course evaluation, and course syllabus. There were 13 science trainee teachers in biology, chemistry, and physics. The data was coded and grouped into four themes: orientations to teaching about teaching science; tension between directive and collaborative teaching modes; tensions of teaching between domain-specific and subject-specific PCK; and PCK in transition states between PCK for 'teaching about teaching science' and 'teaching science'	There were four themes from the findings (Fig. 1). The self-study approach offered the teacher educator-researcher to understand the limitations of the participant's PCK for teaching science teachers esp. knowledge of teaching strategies and knowledge of assessment of the trainees' learning and relating views and beliefs into teaching. Regarding teaching subject-specific pedagogy and domain-specific pedagogy, the tension prompted the educator to reassess the PCK and teaching groups of teachers from different sciences. This covered trainee teachers' teaching strategies in specific science subjects, and sciences. The other finding covered teacher-centred and student-centred pedagogy where it involved more than just telling and listening but be good role models in teaching. Lastly, this self-study offered contributions for institutional and collective self-study research in teacher education through viewing teacher educators' PCK
25. Goodwin et al. (2014) What Should Teacher Educators Know and Be Able to Do?	This US article referred to a study of teacher educators concerning the foundation elements of their practices, evaluation of their preparation, and how the findings informed their preparation as teacher educators. The article used Cochran-Smith and Lytle's (1999) 'relationships of knowledge and practice' to analyse knowledge pertinent to 'teacher educating'. The findings suggested that practising teacher educators felt unprepared to assume their role. However, they could provide insights into preparing teacher educators	The literature review centred on three themes: know-how and ability to do as teacher educators, becoming a teacher educator and the theoretical framework of teacher educator learning by Cochran-Smith and Lytle's (1999, p. 249) 'relationships of knowledge and practice'. The article focused on Cochran-Smith and Lytle's (1999) framework as it provided three concepts of teacher learning: knowledge-for-practice (formal and external, e.g., content/subject, learning theories and pedagogy), knowledge-in-practice (practical and internal, e.g., embedded in practice and reflection), and knowledge-of-practice (generated by research, i.e., connecting the above two forms of knowledge). The framework is applied to teachers and teacher educators	The project employed a mixed-method approach of an online questionnaire of 45 items using a 5-point Likert scale focusing on theoretical knowledge, its application, content knowledge, ability to conduct research, interpersonal skills, reflection, and professional activities. It also used semi-structured interviews to discuss the survey items. The project drew from 293 university teacher educators	From the findings, knowledge-for-practice included theoretical and content knowledge (e.g., learning theories, models of teaching, and educational philosophy). These university teacher educators saw themselves as specialist teachers of disciplinary knowledge. The status of these educationists was low. Their previous teaching experiences might not be translatable to pedagogy for teacher educating. Knowledge-in-practice lacked consistency. Terms like 'learning through doing', 'sinking or swimming' and 'trial by fire' were used to describe this process. The project raised questions about the preparation of these teacher educators. The findings suggested a need to ascertain the pedagogy of teacher educators that covered learning about teaching and teaching about teaching. Knowledge-in-teaching ought to be an aim for preparing teacher educators. There should be greater research emphasis on the activities of these educators as part of 'knowledge-of-practice'. Underpinning the above pedagogy should be diversity, social justice and multiculturalism

(continued)

Table 5.1 (continued)

Author, year and title	Description of the study	Theoretical underpinnings	Methodology	Significant findings
26. Goodwin and Kosnik (2013) Quality teacher educators = quality teachers	This US article focuses on compulsory teacher educators and assumes that the provision of quality teacher education requires quality teacher educators. The research questions are: What should teacher educators know and how should they be prepared to be those educators. The article is structured as follows: (1) it discusses the policy context in the US in relation to these teacher educators; (2) it relates to areas of knowledge; and (3) it compares how pre-service teachers and novice teacher educators become teachers and educators respectively. Drawing on relevant literature sources, the article argues that teaching is complex, and that teacher education needs to be conceptualised as holistic and integrated. Moreover, the related knowledge should be inquiry-based and focus on problem-solving. On the issue of teacher educator preparation, the article states that this question can only be answered if there is a common agreement on formal preparation and induction	The first part of the literature review focused on the policy contexts of teacher education in the US. The next part deals with preparing quality teacher educators (linchpins in educational reforms (Cochran-Smith 2003). The final part of this literature review was on teaching knowledge	This article is not empirically based	The discussion section provided five knowledge domains (Goodwin 2010). They are personal knowledge/autobiography and teaching philosophy; contextual knowledge of learners, schools and society; pedagogical knowledge/content, theories, teaching methods and curriculum development; sociological knowledge/diversity, cultural relevance and social justice; and social knowledge/cooperative, democratic group process and conflict resolution. Contextual knowledge for novice teacher educators meant understanding the classrooms, teaching institutions and communities. Pedagogical knowledge relates to a curriculum where content, theories and teaching methods are crucial. Teacher educators need to have the sociological knowledge to transform their trainee teachers (and ultimately learners) into reflective citizens to enhance diversity and equality. For the authors, social knowledge means training new teachers to make a difference to their young chargers/learners to create a better world. This transformative activity of teacher educators is a political act
27. Hamilton and Pinnegar (2015) Knowledge as a Teacher Educator	In this US-based book chapter, the authors aimed to explore teacher educator knowledge comprised and ways of obtaining it. The related sections were knowing as teacher educators, embodied knowing and identity, practical knowing, and teacher educators' personal practical knowledge. The authors suggested that teacher educator's knowledge, and identity were connected and achieved through experiences and development of embodied	The theoretical frameworks used in the literature review focused on three aspects. They included teacher educators' knowing, identity, and practical reasoning. Regarding knowing, Clandinin's (1985) personal practical knowledge was used to discuss knowledge of teacher educators. Regarding identity formation, language used in articulating our life and experiences provide us with meanings (Lakoff and Johnson 1980). With practical reasoning, Stern (2004) provided a way of unpacking our embodied knowledge by creating narratives of our routines (e.g., observation of a student teacher). Fenstermacher (1986) offered another approach by examining an action to reveal beliefs and knowledge	This was a theoretical delineation of the two teacher educators' experiences	The authors argued that teacher educators' actions, such as curriculum design, was related to their personal practical knowledge. Their understanding of politics in educational institutions was based on practical, tacit and embodied knowledge as teacher educators. The knowledge was dynamic as it could shift, expand, and integrate into our experiences. A teacher educator was informed by contexts and situations relating to one's actions and practices. These contextual actions and experiences shaped one's identity, thus idiosyncratic and individualistic

(continued)

Table 5.1 (continued)

Author, year and title	Description of the study	Theoretical underpinnings	Methodology	Significant findings
28. Hanley and Thompson (2021) 'Generic pedagogy is not enough': Teacher educators and subject-specialist pedagogy in the Further Education and Skills sector in England	This study focused on the preparation of teacher educators in the Further Education and Skills (FE) sector in England. 36 teacher educators participated in this interventionist methodological approach of workshops (i.e., mini-lectures, group activities and resources), survey, and telephone interviews. The study aimed to understand subject-specialist pedagogy using a socially constructed pedagogical content knowledge perspective. The findings offered a typology for a longer-term sustainability of its impact	The aim of this interventionist study was to support teacher educators in developing subject-specialist pedagogy of trainee teachers. The authors conceptualised subject-specialist pedagogy in the following ways. The sector viewed professional knowledge as subject knowledge (Robson 2006) with "a particular mistrust of pedagogy" (p. 2). They referred to Bernstein's (1996) construction of pedagogy consisting of knowledge, values and behaviour, and referred to Bernstein's classification of pedagogical content knowledge (i.e., strong and weak) and subject-specialist (i.e., visible and invisible forms) provision. Shulman's (1987) typology of teaching knowledge was referred, especially, pedagogical content knowledge	The project used an interventionist methodological approach to understand teacher educators' perspectives of subject-specific pedagogy. The assumptions behind this approach were PCK and related concepts could redress this deficiency, and greater understanding of PCK amongst teacher educators could facilitate their delivery teaching education courses The interventionist method composed of workshops (lectures, group activities and online materials), survey and telephone interviews. The participants consisted of two groups with sizes of 15 and 21, from universities and FE colleges. The data analysis focused on organisation of SSP, teacher educators' prior knowledge, characteristics of SSP and vale of intervention	The findings covered three aspects: awareness and short-term impact, barriers to adoption, and longer-term impact Regarding the first aspect, the diversity of subject specialism (e.g., childcare, engineering and manufacturing, and hair and beauty) was an issue for developing subject-specialist content. The second aspect revolved round tensions introducing new ideas about subject-specialist pedagogy within current generic ITE courses. Other issues included barriers to implementation, and low priority given to pedagogical development. The third aspect on longer-term impact, there was no resounding results. Intervention impact could be diminished as well as embedded in practice The findings suggested participants valued acquiring subject-specific pedagogy knowledge with the possibility of translation into practice
29. Hood and Littlejohn (2017) Knowledge typologies for professional learning: educators' (re)generation of knowledge when learning open educational practice	This UK-centred empirically based mixed methods study centred on open education resources (OER) and open education practices (OEP) and their implications for teacher educators. The findings included the identification of six knowledge types of know-how and that these educators needed multiple types of knowledge and use them interchangeably	"Open education practices (OEP) are defined as practices which support the (re)use and production of OER through institutional policies, promote innovative pedagogical models, and respect and empower learners as co-producers on their lifelong learning path" (p. 1585 in Conole and Ehlers 2010; OPAL 2011) These pedagogic activities took place with socio-cultural and socio-regulative knowledge Tynjälä's (2008) model of integrated pedagogies for professional expertise. The mediating tools in Tynjälä's model become key resources in the construction of socio-cultural knowledge" (p. 1587)	There were two phases in this project. Phase 1, data was gathered using a modified version of a validated instrument for evaluating self-regulated learning in occupational practice. It consisted of 521 educators (mainly from universities) across Europe using a survey. The survey covered six factors: experimenting in practice, planning and goal setting, self-efficacy, self-reflection, interaction with others, and learning value. This data capture was followed by 30 semi-structured interviews to ascertain the participants' behaviour and actions in the workplaces and their conceptualisation of their learning Phase 2 studied how educators learned from and with OER Following a series of analytical processes, six knowledge types were identified	The findings discussed the identified six knowledge types from the data analysis. These were general theoretical knowledge; specific theoretical knowledge; practical/ experiential knowledge; self-regulative knowledge; socio-cultural knowledge (community-based); and socio-cultural knowledge (workplace-based) The findings showed two significant components for educators' professional development. One related to accessing multiple forms of knowledge to move fluidly among new practices, and two, they needed to evolve their practices different knowledge types to evolve their practices

(continued)

Table 5.1 (continued)

Author, year and title	Description of the study	Theoretical underpinnings	Methodology	Significant findings
30. Jegstad et al. (2022) Dichotomous and Multifaceted: Teacher Educators' Understanding of Professional Knowledge in Research-based Teacher Education	This Nordic-based article focused on teacher educators' professional knowledge in research-based teacher education. Based on interviews of 16 Norwegian and six Finnish teacher educators, the study found two categories of professional knowledge. They included academic characteristics and personal characteristics. Additionally, three dichotomies were featured. These were educational sciences versus subject sciences, research versus teaching, and collaboration versus autonomy. The dichotomous and multifaceted professional knowledge provided a platform for professional development of teacher education in the two Nordic countries	The literature review consisted of two parts: overview of research on teacher education and related concepts. Three aspects of professional development were raised by researchers regarding induction phase of becoming a teacher educator (Murray and Male 2005), identity (Izadinia 2014), and professional development (Flores 2018). Further significant aspects of these educators' professional development (Luneberg et al. 2014) included context (i.e., professional standards), personal qualities (e.g., intrinsic motivation, and support and research (e.g., lack of time and resources (Ping et al. 2018)) Concerning teacher educators' professional knowledge, it is multifaceted (Aspfors et al. 2019), Smith and Flores (2019) viewed this knowledge as teacher educators' professional expertise and teachers' professional expertise. Smith and Ulvik (2015) these educators' professional knowledge as covering content knowledge, communicative knowledge, knowledge regarding adult learning, feedback, research knowledge and development of reflective ability with others. Other researchers (e.g., Tack and Vanderlinde 2014; Korthagen et al. 2005; Hökkä et al. 2017) placed greater emphasis on research due to the academisation of these educators	This project was part of a larger study using semi-structured interviews. 16 teacher educators from two Norwegian universities and six educators from a Finnish university participated. They had diverse subject and educational backgrounds and job titles. The interviews were transcribed, and their contents analysed	The results provided two main categories (i.e., academic and professional characteristics) and six sub-categories of teacher educators' knowledge (i.e., methodological and research skills, critical and analytical skills, and dissemination and use of research for academic characteristics, and change competence, perception of knowledge types, and collaboration for personal characteristics) in research-focused teacher education programmes. The findings offered limited consensus among the participants regarding their understanding of professional knowledge (Berry 2007; Loughran 2006) From these findings, three dichotomies were ascertained. They included education sciences versus subject sciences, research versus teaching, and teaching versus research

(continued)

Table 5.1 (continued)

Author, year and title	Description of the study	Theoretical underpinnings	Methodology	Significant findings
31. John (2002) The teacher educator's experience: case studies of practical professional knowledge	This UK-based study focused on teacher educators' roles, knowledge and understandings with student teachers. Six teacher educators delivering on a teacher education programme at a British university participated in this qualitative study consisting of life history narratives, semi-structured interviews, observations of classroom delivery and document research	The literature review section started with a discussion of defining teacher educators by researchers such as Ducharme (1986), Jackson (1975), Roemer and Martinello (1982), Finklestein (1984), Ducharme and Agne (1982) and Lanier and Little (1985). The researchers adopted Lanier and Little's (1985, p. 77) definition as "those whose main responsibility it is for the delivery of subject methods courses and professional studies inputs and supervising the practicum, who most readily identify themselves as teacher educators". This study used practical and personal practical knowledge by Elbaz (1983), Clandinin (1986), and Connelly and Clandinin (1988). The knowledge types covered principles (e.g., beliefs and values), and practice rules (e.g., observed, and formulated statements of action in specific learning contexts) (p. 325)	Six teacher educators from a UK teacher education programme in a UK higher education institution participated in this qualitative study. Life history narratives, semi-structured interviews, lesson observations and related documents (e.g., handbooks, resources and materials) were gathered and analysed. An interpretive synthesis was employed to offer a generalisable approach	The findings provided two 'case studies' of Beth and Edward to provide deep understanding of practical professional knowledge of the teacher educators. Five overarching themes arose: (1) Intentionality of the educators, (2) practicality ethics (as espoused by Doyle and Ponder 1977), (3) subject specificity of the educators' knowledge, (4) sense of ethicality (Freidson 1970) The authors defined teacher educators' roles as "passing on a set of traditions based on principled thought and action, which defined the life of the teacher and the taught" (p. 339)
32. Karim (2021) Bridging the Gaps between Teacher Educators and Student Teachers' Perceptions about the Attributes of Effective Teacher Educators	This quantitative study of 334 student teachers and 74 teacher educators in Indonesia examined the attributes of effective EFL teacher educators into four categories: subject matter knowledge (SMK), pedagogic knowledge (PK), organisation and communication skills (OCS), and socio-affective skills (SAS). The findings suggested the two groups of participants had different perceptions of SMK, PK and OCS with no significantly varied SAS	The authors started with the assumption effective teacher educators possessed specific attributes related to knowledge (Dincer et al. 2013; Cheung 2006; Thompson et al. 2004). Park and Lee (2006) offered three knowledge categories: subject matter knowledge, pedagogical knowledge, and socio-affective skills. These attributes were supported by the Indonesian National Ministry of Education Regulation (2007), responsible for setting standards to evaluate teachers' academic qualifications and competences	The online questionnaire adopted from Park and Lee's (2006) study focused on four attributes: SMK, PK, OCS, and SAS. The Indonesia-wide higher education institutions sampled 408 EFL teacher educators using a four-point Likert scale questions	The findings resulted in the following observations. Regarding subject matter knowledge, the teacher educators/participants had higher perceptions regarding this knowledge type than student teachers. Competence of SMK (i.e., knowledge of language and language components) was perceived as important by teacher educators. Regarding PK, teacher educators gave higher mean scores in this knowledge than student teachers With SAS, student teachers provided higher mean score than teacher educators. SAS covered positive interactions with trainee teachers (Berline 2000). Both participating groups viewed motivating and supporting students' emotional wellbeing as significant (Park and Lee 2006)

(continued)

Table 5.1 (continued)

Author, year and title	Description of the study	Theoretical underpinnings	Methodology	Significant findings
33. Katyal and Pang (2010) Paradigms, perspectives and dichotomies amongst teacher educators in Hong Kong	This Hong Kong-based study investigated local and foreign teacher educators' concepts, beliefs and understandings. It argued that 'good practice' might be compromised after accounting for Confucianism dimension. The findings suggested that was the case and that future teacher educators needed to recontextualise good practice from a Confucianism perspective	The authors referred to Shulman's (1986) pedagogical content knowledge (PCK) model as a construct of 'good practice' drawing together constructivist and egalitarian concepts. The authors argued Confucianism affected Hong Kong's educational system. This cultural dimension and self-identity (Bodycott 1997) affected teaching practice. These dimensions in an era of international education could cause deliverers to question and adapt their pedagogical approaches, which Bates called 'defensible theory of education' (Bates 2008, p. 286)	This project used University of Hong Kong as a higher education institution to sample 8 teacher educators with compulsory school education experiences. The participants taught on in-service and pre-service teacher education programmes. Of the eight participants, all were Chinese, bar two from abroad. An interpretative methodological approach was applied using semi-structured interviews, video recordings and observational data	The qualitative findings were thematically topologized into the following sections. They included: (1) role modelling versus learner autonomy, (2) role-modelling as an affective exercise, (3) different perspective, (4) developing teacher knowledge versus critically engaging with knowledge, and 5, passive learners versus engaged learners. The findings offer some implications. They include viewing contextual complexities in its entirety, requiring higher educational institutions to re-conceptualise their pedagogical models, acknowledging teacher educators were influenced by social and educational antecedents, learning by students were culturally driven, and connecting trainee teachers' learning in teacher education courses and their classroom practices

(continued)

Table 5.1 (continued)

Author, year and title	Description of the study	Theoretical underpinnings	Methodology	Significant findings
34. Kidd et al. (2022) Reflexivity for Whom? The Ethics of a Craft Identity and the Know-How of Supporting Reflexivity on Teacher Education Programmes	This research monograph chapter revisits the concept of 'craft' and uses Sennett's (2008) 'The Craftsman' to explore how teacher educators facilitate the development of teacher trainees' craft. The chapter also investigates how VET professionals are supported to become teacher educators. In so doing, this double hermeneutic (the craft of the teacher and the craft of the teacher educator) is discussed using reflectivity. The empirical data was derived from the 2019 InFo-TED study, a pan-European professional development project that explored teacher educators' learning. This study used two narrative case studies of VET educationists as new teacher educators. It raises issues concerning know-how and reflectivity of boundary-crossers into the teacher educator professional area. The boundary-crossing participants are FE trainees moving from their own VET settings to training to teach their specialist subjects. The other group of boundary crossers is teacher educators transferring from teaching VET in FE to university-based teacher education. Thus, the chapter investigates "professionalism as reformed and reframed by recent policy discourse and the means in which FE ITE might harness a renewed professionalism to speak about an ethical orientation of craft". (p. 106)	The chapter uses Sennett's (2006) concept of craft from the perspectives of place and space in the modern industrial world. Sennett invoked city and urban ecology of lives, identity and relationships, and the politics of community, togetherness, and cooperation. Sennett analysed the working lives of people living and working in the work environments of advanced capitalist countries. Sennett then provided a concept of craft working that encouraged thinking, creativity, and self-reflectivity. His view of culture and related practices are based on the ideas by Marx and Bourdieu. Sennett's (2008, p. 9) definition of craft included the "desire to do a job well for its own sake." Thus, a VET teacher educator seeks to support trainee teachers to become teachers through practice, guidance, and support; and for Sennett (2008), this process involved ethics and the achievement of quality work, which would be the 'primordial mark of identity'. This chapter rested its conceptualization through the ethical perspective. This part of the literature review on reflectivity rested on researchers such as Dewey (1916), Schon (1987) (with his reflection-on-action), Zeichner's (1999) new scholarship within teacher education', and Archer (2012) (where reflection is reflexive at the point when internal processes alter belief). In this chapter, reflectivity is applied to boundary-crossing practices in two ways. One is novice teacher educators moving into higher education teacher training programmes (second-order practitioners). Two relates to novice teachers in FE (first-order practitioners)	The International Forum for Teacher Educator Development (InFo-TED) project group was the platform for creating this chapter. Representatives were drawn from Belgium, England, Israel, Ireland, The Netherlands, Norway, Scotland, and the USA. There was funding to run a summer school in 2018. An outcome of this activity resulted in this chapter. The study relied on two narrative case studies. The English participants were VET teacher educators who were new to their roles	There are four examples of the analysed narrative accounts: 'zipper jam', anxieties and fears at boundary-crossing, meaningful reflective practices—future proofing, and moving on and working on identity 'Zipper jam' is illustrated by the two case studies, which results from "conflict, unease, problematisation and brings us to a pedagogical discomfort zone triggering a heightened self-awareness and close reflection. I can learn so much during this discomfort as I put in all my energy to solve the problem and to make the zipper work". The zipper jam notion, as shown previously, exemplified Sennett's (2008) idea of higher processes of skill which involved tacit knowledge (as an anchor) and self-conscious awareness (as critique and corrective). The participants were 'pulled in contrary directions'. This term has implications for these professionals' identity formation and boundary crossing, and the reflective practices might enrich teacher trainees' learning Teacher educators in higher education experienced anxieties and fears in performing their second-order professional roles. They questioned their beliefs and assumptions, which might be destabilising. However, these emotions are also felt by novice teachers. Part of the anxiety and fear referred to the uncertainty of knowledge to use crossing boundaries, thus affecting the participants' identity formation. They found that having supportive colleagues and mentors was crucial in negotiating this crossing The collaborative activity was seen as a 'unifying bond' for future professional development. The project facilitated this development. The activity enabled these professionals to generate resilience or 'pedagogic agility' to perform well as teacher educators The 'ripple effects of professional learning during boundary crossing supported the participants' 'situational self'. These effects affected their identity constructions and to strive for quality

(continued)

Table 5.1 (continued)

Author, year and title	Description of the study	Theoretical underpinnings	Methodology	Significant findings
35. Kosnik et al. (2015) Four spheres of knowledge required: an international study of the professional development of literacy/English teacher educators	This international study in Canada, US, England, and Australia of 28 literacy teacher educators (LTE) centred on professional development, informal, formal and communities of practice, and knowledge types pertaining to research, pedagogy of higher education, literacy and literacy teaching, and current school location and government initiatives. The study revealed the complexity of knowledge and identified three professional development activities in teacher education	The literature review section referred to the Green Paper on Teacher Education in Europe (Buchberger et al. 2006) as a starting basis of teacher educators' professional development. Lunenberg et al. (2014) suggested six roles of teacher educators, but activities regarding professional development appeared neglected
Professional development appeared contested with varying definitions from sources, such as Hardy (2012), Earley and Porritt (2010), Bubb and Early (2007) and Schon (1983)
Concerning knowledge types, Goodwin (2008) identified five types: personal, contextual, pedagogical, sociological, and social. Performative management, politicisation, and commodification of education (Sachs and Mockler 2012; Ellis et al. 2013; Holbrook 2004) were issues identified in this review
Three forms of professional development—formal, informal and community of practice—were identified (Griffiths et al. 2010; Boyd and Harris 2010; Wenger et al. 2002). Four spheres of knowledge based on research, pedagogy of higher education, literacy and teaching, and current school and government initiatives were reviewed (Livingston et al. 2009; Murray 2010; Williams et al. 2012; Murray and Male 2005; Gee and Hayes 2011; Bayer 2009; Nixon et al. 2012)	The two research questions in this study focused on the knowledge types that LTEs require and forms of professional development that LTEs used
The international study used a snowball sampling approach to capture empirical data from the eventual 28 Literacy teacher educators. Teacher educators from English-speaking countries—Canada, US, UK and Australia—were targeted. Only LTEs with doctorate qualifications with compulsory school teaching experiences were asked. Two semi-structured interviews were used to gather qualitative data. NVivo software was employed to analyse the data covering coding, quotations, annotations, and memos	The findings covered four knowledge themes on research, pedagogy of higher education, literacy and its teaching, and current school and government initiatives
Regarding higher education pedagogy, participants were committed to improving their pedagogical knowledge. The novice LTEs relied on feedback from their student teachers to understand their teaching effectiveness. For more experienced LTEs, observations were more relevant for their trainee teachers' learning
On literacy and related teaching, the study found three professional development activities. These were informal, formal and communities of practice: covering networking, participating on research teams, attending conferences and external academic networks, fostering school-based partnerships, involving in teacher associations, and reading journals
Lastly, LTEs had issues juggling their education visions with government initiatives

(continued)

Table 5.1 (continued)

Author, year and title	Description of the study	Theoretical underpinnings	Methodology	Significant findings
36. Kumar (2021) Technological Pedagogical Content Knowledge of Educators of Teacher Education Program Working in Colleges of Education	This study based in India focused on the relationships between teacher educators of a teacher education programme and their gender, taught subjects, age and teaching experiences regarding the technological pedagogical content knowledge (TPACK). A survey was used to gather empirical data. The findings indicated that there was no significant influence of the teacher educators' teaching experiences in their TPACK	Luik et al.'s (2018) and Housseini and Anand (2013) studies found significant differences between the gender regarding technological content knowledge. In a broader study by Cetin-Berber and Erdem (2015), they found significant difference among pre-service teachers' views of technological pedagogical content knowledge in relation to gender, programme, and experience. Research conducted by ShibliNaaz et al. (2018) identified differences in their technological knowledge but not TPACK knowledge and gender	This study used a questionnaire to gather data of 136 teacher educators of a teacher education course. The survey consisted of seven knowledge domains that supported content-based technology applied in teaching. Its aim was to ascertain any significant difference between gender, taught subjects, age group, and teaching experiences. Statistical measures, such as mean, standard deviation, 'T' test, variance, and regression analysis, were employed in discussing the findings	The six findings included no significant in four areas. They included genders of these teacher educators in their technological knowledge, teaching of subjects and pedagogy subjects in their technological knowledge, technological pedagogical knowledge, technological content knowledge and technological pedagogical content knowledge. The other two areas were age groups of these educators regarding the four technological know-how and their teaching experiences However, there were significant differences in two areas: gender and the technological knowledge types, and taught subjects and pedagogy subjects regarding pedagogical knowledge, content knowledge, and pedagogical content knowledge

(continued)

Table 5.1 (continued)

Author, year and title	Description of the study	Theoretical underpinnings	Methodology	Significant findings
37. Loo (2020) Professional Development of Teacher Educators in Further Education	This research monograph is the first evidence-based investigation of teacher educators in the English further education sector. The five main research questions are: 1. What are the routes to becoming a teacher educator in the sector? 2. How do teacher educators train others to become teachers? 3. What knowledge(s) do they draw on and apply in their work? 4. How do they maintain their professional development? 5. How do they view themselves? The eight researchers from FE teacher educators in England used the following research methods to collect data. These include a survey, one-to-one semi-structured interviews, documentary research and 'Talking Heads'. The 33 participants were drawn from teacher educators teaching in FE colleges, universities and private providers The nine chapters began with an introduction to the English FE sector with its characteristics, the research questions and methodology, and the structure of the book. Chapter 2 provided readers with an overview of the recent history of teacher education and teacher professionalism in this English FE sector. The following chapter contained the participants' profiles of the survey. These profiles included gender, age group, first and other languages, academic and professional qualifications, current job descriptions, previous jobs and a 7-point Likert scale on their professional identity. This information is used in the remaining chapters of the book. Chapter 4 explored participants' pathways to becoming teacher educators. The next chapter looked at their knowledge (types and sources) and application in training student teachers. Chapter 6 looked at their professional identity and the following chapter explored their professional training. Chapter 8 contained three case studies of the participants, one from each of the three teaching settings. The final chapter concludes the monographic study with sections on connections between themes and omissions, areas for further research and implications of this book	The relevant chapters are C2 on Teacher Education, C4 Ways of Teacher Education, C5 Knowledge of Teacher Educators, C6 Professional Identities and C7 Professional Education The relevant literature sources in C4 are Becher (1994), Klein (1996) and Tight (2015). The relevant sources in C5 on teacher educators' knowledge are included in the next listing in this table (Loo, forthcoming 2024). In C6, the relevant sources include identities by Gee (2000–2001), Sfard and Prusak (2005) and McKeon and Harrison (2010). Professionalism has been defined by these researchers. These include Lave and Wenger (1991), Boyd and Harris (2010), Bullough (2005), McGregor et al. (2010), Boyd et al. (2010), White (2011), Murray et al. (2011), Pereira et al. (2015), Swennen et al. (2010), Loo (2019) and Zembylas (2007). In the final chapter on professional development, appropriate literature sources for novice teacher educators were Boyd (2010), Murray (2005), Velzen et al. (2010), Davey and Ham (2010), Boyd et al. (2011) and White (2013). For professional development of existing teacher educators, the relevant sources were Knight et al. (2014), Loughran (2014), O'Dwyer and Atli (2015), Barak et al. (2010), Exley and Ovenden-Hope (2013), Hilton et al. (2013), Boei et al. (2015), Yaffe and Maskit (2010, Griffiths et al. (2010), McGregor et al. (2010, and Willemse et al. (2016)	The methodological procedure was included in the appendix. In it were the five research questions, the eight investigators, the research methods (survey, interviews, documentary research and Talking Heads), anonymised details of the 33 participants, a table showing the relationships between the research questions, the survey, the interview questions and the Talking Heads, the letter of introduction, the informed consent form, the questionnaire, the interview questions, the guidelines for the 'Talking Heads' and the guidelines for the co-researchers as participants in the project Purposive sampling was employed through related national networks such as the Teacher Educators UK, the Learning and Skills Research Network and the British Educational Research Association Post-compulsory and Lifelong Learning SIG. The Principal Investigator's institution—University College London—approved the ethical application. Before collecting data from the 33 participants, a pilot study was conducted. This project used an audit trail approach, linking the details of a participant's completed survey, interview, and Talking Head recording, and looking for commonalities between the data analysed from each of the data sources. This approach was then applied to the analysis, synthesis and detailing of the relevant data for use in the chapters in the research monograph. Triangulation within the analysed data was carried out as well as between the sources. Thus, an intra- and inter-analytical approach was used for each participant's data to look for commonalities and differences between data sources. In this way, the analysis sought to ensure consistency and academic and research credibility	The findings of the C2 study on teacher education show that various government policies have attempted to define and redefine professionalism in the teaching profession. These may be summarised as a dominant discourse on education and training by a neoliberal philosophy that created an imbalance of power between teachers and the state. It prioritised compliance over critique and characterised the teaching profession by professional competence rather than professional knowledge. The professional status of FE teachers was that of a poor cousin compared to compulsory education teachers. The FE teachers' willingness to handle a larger workload, including emotional labour for their students, as well as the bureaucratic and administrative demands of their jobs, mask their rejection of the neoliberal business model of education In the ways of becoming FE teacher educators, C4 has indicated three major (and nine minor) ways. As for the study on current titles, it reflected the roles of these educators, which are broadly divided into frontline and managerial roles. There are also sectoral differences between those working in FE, and higher education and in the private sector C5 on teacher educators' knowledge defined it broadly to encompass knowledge, experience, abilities, attitudes, and skill sets. The sources and forms of knowledge were identified. The three-level conceptual framework provided a complex picture of the knowledge and applications of these FE teacher educators. The use of recontextualization processes provided a dynamic, changing and transforming picture of these educators' experiences, which are constantly changing. These experiences change and transform them as people and teacher educators In relation to professional identities, four themes were identified in the findings. These include professionalism, attributes and pedagogy, emotional connection, and contextual issues The final chapter on professional development focused on two needs of novice and experienced teacher educators. Despite their different pedagogical experiences, there were commonalities. These included pedagogy, emotional connection, and informal approaches to professional development, mentoring and research capabilities. In England, there were no structured and specific courses for these educators. However, the abolition of mandatory teaching qualifications in the Lingfield report does not contribute to the professionalisation of teachers in this sector. However, four themes were identified for the professional development of the novice and experienced educators (as mentioned earlier). The two overarching dimensions were individual and collaborative approaches to professional development, and external and internal ways of ensuring such activities

Table 5.1 (continued)

Author, year and title	Description of the study	Theoretical underpinnings	Methodology	Significant findings
38. Loughran and Berry (2005) Modelling by teacher educators	This article focuses on modelling by teacher educators by investigating the nature and development of explicit modelling by two educationists about an Australian preservice education course. It found that via collaborative self-study, they conceptualized a teacher education pedagogy using learning through the experience of 'being explicit'	The literature review relied on self-study of teacher education practices to study teacher educators' knowledge and pedagogy. Kosnik (2001) viewed self-study as an approach by teacher educators mirroring their teaching trainee teachers. Hamilton and Pinnegar (1998) argued self-study, where the researcher/teacher provided evidence, they knew what they claimed to know	Using self-study as a methodological approach, the authors applied a longitudinal focus by collaborating. They used their experiences and data sources (e.g., journals) to explore explicit modelling at two levels. The first relates to their teaching trainees for them to enact them in their teaching sessions. The next level referred to offering their trainees access to pedagogical reasoning, emotions, reflections, and enactments in different teaching and learning contexts	The authors used Korthagen et al.'s (2001) episteme and phronesis conceptualizations for teaching. Episteme refers to using expert knowledge to solve a problem, whereas phronesis concerns practical wisdom in understanding a complex and specific situation. When applied to teacher education, there are times when issues from practical experience may not be resolved using theoretical know-how. They argued that 'pedagogic interventions' in 'living through' experiences provided real learning about teaching. They used tensions in teaching and learning about teaching to conceptualize the complexity of modelling teaching. The essence of modelling is laying bare a teacher educator's pedagogical thoughts and actions for critique and facilitate student-teachers' learning about teaching. A lone teacher educator might feel vulnerable without the support of a peer in modelling enactments They argued that a knowledge of practice (of teacher educators) in teaching about teaching is crucial in understanding their roles and know-how. They identified four areas of practice in this knowledge of modelling. They included: (1) critiquing that offered ways of seeing into experience and (2) viewing different teaching decisions in action underlined teaching tensions. The other two areas are (3) highlighting variations of action and intent provide new ways of viewing teaching practices, and (4) valuing collaboration and co-teaching stimulates new teaching possibilities

(continued)

Table 5.1 (continued)

Author, year and title	Description of the study	Theoretical underpinnings	Methodology	Significant findings
39. Mork et al. (2021) Defining knowledge domains for science teacher educators	The theoretical study carried in Norway focused on science teacher educators' (STEs) knowledge domains. The findings gave an updated theorisation of STEs' knowledge and qualifications alongside other factors including deep learning, critical thinking skills, cross-curricular working, sustainable development, and research-based teacher education. The four knowledge domains were used as a tool to ascertain needs, staff recruitment and professional development	The discussion column provided the pertinent literature sources and related discussions	No empirical data was used in this article	The foci of this conceptual article included the need for conceptualising science teacher educators' (STEs) knowledge and qualifications and developing professional studies especially for those future-oriented science teacher education. The authors proposed four knowledge domains covering natural science, science education in school, science teacher education and science education research. For natural science domain, the relevant knowledge included subject matter, content knowledge, knowledge of research practices and understanding of the Nature of Science (Osborne 2014; Abd-El-Khalick and Lederman 2000; Allchin 2017; Hodson and Wong 2017; Futak et al. 2012). Regarding the second domain on science education in school, the knowledge types included relevant learning theories, their application to student learning, school science curriculum, teaching strategies, inquiry-based science education, use of assessment, promotion of twenty-first century skills in science and organisation of cross-curricular work and sustainable development of science education. The related literature sources were Lederman et al. (1997), Leach and Scott (2003), Abell et al. (2009), Windschitl et al. (2018), Baxter et al. (2004), Biggs and Tang (2011), OECD (2019), Munkebye et al. (2020), and Evans et al. (2017). The third domain focused on science teacher education. The types of knowledge included modelling research-based teaching practices, pre- and in-service teachers as learners, and support pre-7 and in-service teachers in implementing educational reforms (Loughran 2014; Lunenberg et al. 2007; Avraamidou 2014). The final domain—science education research—include knowledge types of educational research approaches, conducting and disseminating science education research, supervising students at master's level, findings, interpreting and applying research findings, and academic writing. The related sources were Lederman et al. (1997), Darling-Hammond (2017), Cochran-Smith (2005), and Czerniawski et al. (2017). The authors suggested the significance of making visible and explicit the knowledge types for STEs to facilitate teacher education. They also provided an awareness of the STEs' roles as professionals in implementing quality and future-oriented science education in schools

(continued)

Methodological Approach   101

Table 5.1 (continued)

Author, year and title	Description of the study	Theoretical underpinnings	Methodology	Significant findings
40. Nagel (2021) Digital Competence in Teacher Education Curricula: What Should Teacher Educators Know, Be Aware of and Prepare Students for?	This Norway-based study used a qualitative methodological approach to study the impact of digitalization on teacher educators' knowledge. The findings focused on teacher educators' pedagogical application of digital tools, and to teacher students the skillset. The study implied that these educators needed an understanding of digitalisation's implications for teacher education practices to facilitate their trainee teachers' digital competence	Two related research questions in this study of local policy documents are: how is digital competence addressed in teacher education curricula at the institutional level, and how are teacher educators expected to be aware of and prepare student teachers for epistemic changes? (p. 105) Mishra and Koehler (2006) propounded the model of technological, pedagogical content knowledge (TPACK) to understand teachers' digital competence (TDC). Later models included Krumsvik's (2014) development of didactical competence and learning strategies; Brevik et al.'s (2019) suggestion of a transformative digital agentic approach; and Ottestad et al.'s (2014) combination of three forms of digital competences: generic, didactical, and professional-oriented Lund and Aagaard (2020) to include the impact of digital technologies in knowledge construction. Lund and Aagaard (2020) identified three approaches that digitalisation impact epistemic practices. These were extended cognition (human interactions with technologies), embedded cognition (ubiquitous of technology in everyday lives), and embodied cognition (impact of digital artefacts on bodies and senses)	This study centred on a five-year teacher education master's course that integrated disciplinary and pedagogical studies (i.e., the concurrent model). The focus of this programme was on children aged 10–15. Six teacher education institutions in Norway were selected, covering 317 local policy documents. The courses included disciplines ranging from Arts and Crafts, English, National Sciences, Pedagogy, Religious and Ethical Studies to Special Needs Education. Documentary analysis (Bowen 2009), alongside a thematic approach (Braun and Clarke 2006) were employed. The researchers used Lund and Aagaard's (2020) abductive methodological approach to categorise the documents. This approach included three perspectives with epistemological implications relating to extended cognition, embedded cognition, and embodied cognition	The findings provided seven themes. They included digital tools, digital didactics and pedagogy, students' basic and digital skills, culture, society and democracy, digital responsibility and ethical awareness, professional digital competences (PDC), and development and transformations. The first theme was the most frequently quoted. The second was related to teaching and learning, and the third theme referred to students' application. The fourth theme related to societal perspective of citizenship, democracy, and digital division. The fifth theme focused on copyright, cyber-ethics, identity, privacy, and etiquette. PDC referred to students' knowledge and their digital competence. The final theme advocated lifelong learning, research of pedagogical application of the technologies, and related transformation of subjects and educational practices. Regarding the policy documents, they focused on digital tools, digital didactics and pedagogy, and students' basic and digital skills. Concerning the disciplines there were variations. Only the natural sciences looked at algorithms, programming, flipped classrooms, simulation, and modelling. Languages focused on digital didactics and pedagogy and digital tools. Religious studies, arts and crafts and physical education centred on digital responsibility Regarding TDC, the policy documents shifted depending on its context. In the intermediate and advanced level, there were greater emphasis on digital didactics and pedagogy category (especially culture, society and democracy, and development and transformation) over digital tools category Regarding explicit texts of the three cognitive forms, the 'extended cognition' included references, such as reflection and awareness of learning with digital tools and general competences (p. 115). With embedded cognition, there were text references to fostering students' ability to live and work as a democratic citizen (p. 115). However, there were no textual expressions relating to embodied cognition

(continued)

Table 5.1 (continued)

Author, year and title	Description of the study	Theoretical underpinnings	Methodology	Significant findings
41. Ohito (2019) Mapping women's knowledges of antiracist teaching in the United States: A feminist phenomenological study of three antiracist women teacher educators	This US study used a feminist phenomenological inquiry from White, Western, androcentric view to investigate antiracist teaching of a multiracial female group. This group comprised of three teacher educators. The participants' knowledge shaped their beliefs and teaching. This pilot study provided further research questions concerning how, what, and why antiracist teacher educators enact their work	Kinloch (2018) theorised antiracist teaching as a 'necessary disruption'. Fundamental to feminist theory was research as a commitment to making visible women's lived experiences (Lentin 1993). Regarding this study, the three feminist issues were generation and legitimising of knowledge, the 'canon' of traditional knowledge, and process and connection (Sarikakis et al. 2009). The author drew on feminist theory and methodology by authors such as Fisher and Embree (2000), de Beauvoir (2011), and Butler (1997). The author identified the following issues of antiracist activity: its teaching (Aveling 2006; Mueller and O'Connor 2007), what to teach (Ulluci 2020; McIntosh 1988; Shalaby 2013; Jett 2012), and rationale for teaching (Case and Jennings 2005; Picower 2009; Bell 2002; King and Chandler 2016; Milner 2007)	This one-person investigation applied a mixed method feminist phenomenological approach of in-depth semi-structured interviews, observations, documents, and writing (via a reflective journal) to gather empirical data. The analysis of the datasets addressed the methodological concepts of credibility and validity	The findings from the three antiracist women teacher educators uncovered three themes regarding their beliefs and teaching. They were race(ism) and family histories, race(ism) and schooling experiences, and race(ism) and embodiment. With family histories, the author suggested that people could unlearn and change, and formation of relationships could intellectualise racism. With school experiences, childhood memories served as a source of knowledge about antiracist teaching. With embodiment for the three teacher educators, embodiment was crucial to antiracist teaching, as expounded by Spinoza's questioning of what could the body do? (Deluze 1990). The author re-focused the question to antiracist teaching by asking how the body could teach and learn from the context of antiracist delivery and how research might radicalise, gendered, classed, and marked the body (p. 8). Regarding the reasons for teaching this topic, the three teacher educators viewed it as a remembrance activity, as a means to creating knowledge. It also served as motivational and memory-making

(continued)

Table 5.1 (continued)

Author, year and title	Description of the study	Theoretical underpinnings	Methodology	Significant findings
42. Ozmantar and Agac (2021) Mathematics teacher educators' knowledge sources in teacher education practices	This Turkey-based study centred on 281 mathematics teacher educators' (MTEs) knowledge sources in their practices. The quantitative findings from a survey covered knowledge sources and their relationships with four variables. These variables included gender, identity, pedagogic experiences and academic ranking. The findings were discussed concerning professional development, notions of learning and knowing, and impact of knowledge sources to teacher education practices	The literature review centred on teacher educators' knowledge sources for teacher education practices, particularly mathematics teacher educators (MTEs), their knowledge and identities, and for MTEs' knowledge sources provided the cornerstone of these educators' 'field-specific expertise' that impacted their prescription of effective mathematics teaching. The researchers viewed MTEs' roles centering on the three areas: research engagement, teaching, and expertise in field-specific knowledge base. Cochran-Smith and Lytle (1999) offered three aspects of teacher learning: knowledge-for-practice (i.e., link between knowledge-for-practice and knowledge-in-practice). For Goodwin et al. (2014), knowledge-for-practice was acquired through teacher education/ training, and knowledge-in-practice experience, based on practice as embedded knowledge), and knowledge-of-practice (i.e., link between knowledge-for-practice and knowledge-in-practice). Knowledge-of-practice could be viewed as teacher education research that educators might be involved. The authors suggested that Goodwin et al. (2014) offered a better narrative of the three-knowledge conceptual framework from the MTEs' perspectives	This study used a questionnaire to gather data from 281 mathematics teacher educators from a Turkish university. The focus of the questionnaire was the participants' knowledge sources with the following variables: academic ranking (such as, professors, associate and assistant professors), gender, teaching experiences in schools and identity. The survey comprised of two sections—(1) identity and teaching experiences, and (2) open-ended questions on the effective teaching and practices. Two researchers were employed to analyse the data. Inductive thematic analysis of the open-ended questions produced descriptive codes and categories with frequencies. Quantitative analysis using SPSS was employed	From the analysed results, 31 knowledge sources were identified. These were classified into the three knowledge types with 9 sources in knowledge-for-practice, 18 to knowledge-in-practice, and 4 to knowledge-of-practice. Pertinent examples of the first knowledge type covered literature readings, educational backgrounds, and official documents. The second type—knowledge-in-practice had five groups. These were experiences, observations, interaction with academics, interaction with pre- and in-service teachers and role models. With knowledge-of-practice, the sources included their own academic activities rather than research-related activity. From the quantitative analysis, female MTEs viewed postgraduate education as a knowledge source significantly more so than men. Those MTEs relied more on literature readings as knowledge sources than the mathematicians, whereas mathematicians depend less on teaching experience as a knowledge source. Concerning academic ranking, doctoral holders, as the academic ranking increased, reliance on literature readings decreased. There was significant association between their experiences and holders of academic titles. Teaching experiences were related to the three knowledge sources. Those with teaching experience considered their experience as knowledge source compared to those without teaching experience (who drew on curricular documents) From these findings, the authors suggested that knowledge sources contribute to MTEs' professional identities, and each of the three knowledge types develop professional identities differently with infinite possible professional selves

(continued)

Table 5.1 (continued)

Author, year and title	Description of the study	Theoretical underpinnings	Methodology	Significant findings
43. Pascual and Contreras (2021) The Pedagogical Knowledge Deployed by a Primary Mathematics Teacher Educator in Teaching Symmetry	This study of a teacher educator in a Spanish university focused on content of primary school teacher education course and ways the educator mediated the content for teaching trainee/prospective teachers. It utilised observation video recording to investigate the pedagogical content knowledge (PCK) and an interview. The analysis provided three types of PCK	The perspective of the researchers related to a broader belief of a mathematics teacher educator's disciplinary knowledge included the interconnections between the various knowledge types in teaching and teacher development. The authors suggested three knowledge types relating to professional knowledge, teaching practices and professional identity. Thus, they subscribed to Feiman-Nemser's (2008) concept of a teacher, which referred to think, feel, and act like teacher The authors discussed the pedagogical knowledge of primary teacher educator as triangulating with the teacher education programme content and prospective teachers (Jaworski 1992). The course content included professional knowledge of thinking and knowing like a teacher, professional identity (i.e., feeling like a teacher) and practices (i.e., acting like a teacher). For teacher educators, their pedagogical knowledge of training content covered knowledge of —how to teach training content, prospective preservice teachers' learning characteristics, and norms and standards for primary teacher education courses	The methodological design centred on a teacher educator of a primary teacher training programme in professional knowledge construction. Lucas, a mathematics teacher education, had nearly 40 years' experience as a researcher. Data captured for this study included a recording of a training session on symmetry, fieldnotes of the session, and a follow-up interview with the participant. The data sources were transcribed and analysed	The results ascertained a list of the educator's pedagogical knowledge covering knowledge of how to teach content, knowledge of prospective reservice teachers (PPT's) learning and knowledge regarding standards and norms of the primary teacher education programme. Some of the 'how to teach' content included different representations of symmetry, choices of nonstandard examples of shapes, reflections on PPTs' errors as training resources with PPTs, and methodological transference from teacher training to primary education. Concerning PPTs' learning, the indicators covered foreseeing PPTs' issues with mathematical content of axial symmetry. PPTs' duality as mathematics students and prospective teachers, and misunderstandings of symmetry that hindered knowledge construction. Regarding the standards and norms, the indicators covered contents of teacher education should begin from a grounded study of primary content and included elements to help unpack mathematical content

(continued)

Methodological Approach

Table 5.1 (continued)

Author, year and title	Description of the study	Theoretical underpinnings	Methodology	Significant findings
44. Ping et al. (2021) Teacher educators' professional learning: perceptions of Dutch and Chinese teacher educators	This Dutch Chinese article focused on teacher educators' learning in their practice. The quantitative study of 583 Chinese and Dutch teacher educators examined the participants' content learning, related activities, and rationale for pursuing these activities. The findings suggested there were positive correlations between professional learning and educational qualifications and identities. Regarding the two groups' perceptions, statistical differences were identified concerning 'research-related' and 'getting input from others', which were context-related	The study (and survey) centred on three aspects. The first aspect included teacher educator content (i.e., pedagogy of teacher education including knowledge and skillsets, research and reflection, professional identity, and knowledge base), activities, and reasons for engaging in this learning. The related sources were Montecinos et al. (2002), Roberts and Weston (2014), Griffiths et al. (2010), Selkrig and Keamy (2015), Dinkelman (2011), and Patrizio et al. (2011) The second aspect on professional learning activities identified four types. They were learning through academic engagement (Tanner and Davies 2009; Kosnik et al. 2015), learning through collaboration (Hadar and Brody 2010; Sharplin 2011), attending professional development courses (Karagiorgi and Nicolaidou 2013; White et al. 2014), and learning through reflection (Capobianco 2007) The third aspect was reasons for learning. The authors identified three reasons: meeting external requirements (Timmerman 2003), personal ambition (Peeraer and Van Petegem 2012; Sharplin 2011), professional role transition (Williams and Ritter 2010)	The research questions in this quantitative study using questionnaires were (1) the perceptions of the Dutch and Chinese teacher educators regarding learning content, learning activities and reasons for pursuing them, (2) relationships of these perceptions to relevant background variables, (3) variations of the two groups of teacher educators concerning their professional learning Digital questionnaires were administered to 218 Dutch teacher educators in 16 universities. In China, 365 teacher educators participated in the online survey from university institutes. The questionnaire went through various stages of development covering formation, consultation of experts, data collection and validation, pilot study, data collection and data analysis	The findings referred to three themes. The first related to teacher educators' views of their learning scales (as per the questionnaire). The highest rated 'focus' scales were for content, which included pedagogy of teacher education, curriculum and research. The learning focus scales related to academic engagement, getting input from others and the lowest scale, reflection. The third and last focus scales on reasons for learning, personal ambition was highest, followed by professional role transition and external requirement The related background variables provided significant differences concerning professional learning. Those with doctoral qualifications viewed research-related activities, learning through academic engagement and reflection higher than those with lower-level qualifications. The participants with dual roles (work and research) rated high the content theme: 'pedagogy of teacher education', research and curriculum, and the learning theme of academic engagement and getting input from others Regarding the two groups of Chinese and Dutch educators, the former group centred on research as their learning content than Dutch educators. Chinese educators also participated in academic and reflective activities more than their Dutch counterparts. The Dutch group focused more than the Chinese group on getting input from others. For the Chinese participants, the reasons for learning were related professional role transition and external requirement Teacher educators from the two groups appeared to have a desire to learn about their profession and that the differences in professional learning related to their work contexts

(continued)

Table 5.1 (continued)

Author, year and title	Description of the study	Theoretical underpinnings	Methodology	Significant findings
45. Selmer et al. (2016) Multilayered knowledge: understanding the structure and enactment of teacher educators' specialized knowledge base	The study by US-based researchers centred on teacher educators' professional development. Focusing on teacher educator knowledge (TEK), its application was investigated. The authors suggested that in preparing teacher educators' professional development activities should recognise, emphasise, and develop their layered understandings (of knowledge of students and teachers) from a contextual perspective	Chauvot (2009) provided a comprehensive literature review of teacher educators' professional development. One of the commonalities is teacher educators' development of specialised knowledge and skillsets. Reflective practice was used (Cochran-Smith 2003; Van Zoest et al. 2006; Wilson 2006). Another was space for collaborative discussions (Sztajn et al. 2006). Others use domain of teacher knowledge (Shulman 1986; Godwin and Kosnik 2013). Godwin and Kosnik drew on their five forms of teacher educator knowledge (TEK). These were personal knowledge (i.e., experiences), contextual knowledge (relating to historical, political, national and local contexts), pedagogical and content knowledge (i.e., understanding of teaching about teaching), sociological knowledge (of race, class, cultural differences and inequality), and social knowledge (i.e., inter and intrapersonal intelligence). This project used the above sources in three ways: as a long-term development to assess experiences and practices, examined specific and generic intersections of expert knowledge (i.e., interdisciplinary domain of TEK), and the focus on university educators in school-based professional development settings	The four team members of teacher educators included two Mathematics specialists, on English educator and one technology and learning specialist. The university programme trained preservice/trainee teachers with partnerships with local schools. The group researched and designed an integrated professional development for teachers. They worked with six teachers and had six meetings in the year. The meetings covered planning, videoed classroom teaching, and design of a professional development session. Data from audio and video recordings all the planning and development sessions, was transcribed and collaboratively analysed for forms of specialised knowledge base and interactions facilitating professional development. Three emerging themes representing pedagogical content knowledge (Shulman 1986), mathematical teaching knowledge (Ball et al. 2008) and context knowledge (Grossman 1990), were analysed	Three main elements were ascertained from the findings. These included content-specific knowledge, general pedagogical knowledge, and context knowledge. In each of these main elements, there were sub-elements. Content-specific knowledge had two sub-types: subject-matter knowledge and pedagogical content knowledge. General pedagogical knowledge contained three sub-elements: knowledge of learners, knowledge of teaching and knowledge of curriculum. Context knowledge also has three sub-elements. These included global, national, and state, and local contexts

(continued)

Methodological Approach   107

Table 5.1 (continued)

Author, year and title	Description of the study	Theoretical underpinnings	Methodology	Significant findings
46. Stillman et al. (2019) From the ground up: cultivating teacher educator knowledge from the situated knowledges of emerging asset-oriented teacher educators	This article from the US focused on new teacher educators' development in a three-year qualitative project. It used an informal space of Frierean Culture Circles and Boalian Theatre of the Oppressed. The study centred on dynamic knowledge, perspectives and tools regarding the educators' learning and practices in schools and university environments. The study set out to improve equity and justice of 'asset-oriented' teacher educators away from 'whiteness'	The study used this premise—guidance and understanding of asset-oriented teacher educators' pedagogical roles—to investigate a critical teaching and learning space centring on concepts by Freire (1970), Souto-Manning (2010) of situated knowledge construction and transmission (Kincheloe and McLaren 2000). Additionally, it prioritized 'equity-oriented transformation' (p. 266) to include knowledge and practices of minority communities to transform teacher education The theoretical literature centred on preparing novice teacher educators via (1) mentorship and immersion (Wilson 2006; Zeichner 2005) and (2) collaborative reflection and research into their own practices (Cochran-Smith 2003; Goodwin and Kosnik 2013; Loughran 2014) This section reviewed Freire's (1970) critical pedagogy that rejected a 'banking' approach of teachers depositing knowledge into learners and argued for an agentic approach to disrupt inequality and transform marginalised societies. Friere advocated knowledge for learners to learn through a process of co- and re-construction of socially situated knowledge for learners to learn through their experiences and related dialogue. The researchers used critical pedagogy to understand teacher educators' work and to advance equity and justice (Sleeter 2017)	This three-year study occurred in a university in America with trainee teacher educators using semi-structured interviews. Through collaborative sessions, the participants (via a facilitator/researcher) seek to address shared issues surrounding the ways teacher education addressed their deficit ideologies regarding minority students. From an initial group of 21 members, 12 further undertook meetings for the next three years with a commitment to equity	The findings (from these sessions ('culture circles' and theatre of the oppressed (TO)) offered four knowledge types. They were (1) understandings of critical pedagogy and sociocultural learning theory of teachers' learning, (2) awareness of how structural identity manifested in teaching and teacher education, and knowledge to disrupt it, (3) knowledge of pedagogical tools for asset-oriented teacher educators, and (4) recognition of the benefits of dispositions among these teacher educators (p. 272) These four knowledge types were dynamic as they evolved with these educators' experiences and their different social pedagogical contexts. The culture circles provided a support system for these participants and enabled them to develop, construct and understand their situated and embodied roles. This system also affected the educators' identities. The culture circles and TO provided spaces to understand and discuss collectively the educators' emerging vulnerabilities and identities

(continued)

Table 5.1 (continued)

Author, year and title	Description of the study	Theoretical underpinnings	Methodology	Significant findings
47. Superfine and Li (2014) Exploring the Mathematical Knowledge Needed for Teaching Teachers	This US-based study focused on teacher educators' knowledge requirements in teaching preservice elementary mathematics teachers. This knowledge understanding was contrasted with similar K-12 mathematics teachers' know-how. The related content programme was for delivering to preservice teachers. The researchers observed various knowledge types in the teacher educators' practices and ascertained how the observed knowledge types were applied and contrasted with knowledge by similar K-12 teachers	The theoretical frameworks in this study focused on Cochran-Smith and Lytle's (1999) knowledge for practice, knowledge of practice and knowledge in practice, the third type for mathematics teacher educators (MTEs). This knowledge type might also be craft knowledge (Schon 1987). Bergsten and Grevholm (2008) suggested preparing teachers to learn from their own practices as reflective practitioners (Dewey 1960). The know-how required for these educators to teach mathematics to teachers (of K-12 level) included disciplinary/mathematical expertise and pedagogical ones (Bergsten and Grevholm 2008). Mason (1998) researching MTEs required three forms of awareness: 'in-action', 'in-discipline' and 'in-counsel' (see Zazkis and Zazkis 2011). For the researchers, MTEs require mathematical content knowledge, and knowledge of how trainee teachers' mathematical content connected with (teaching) practice. In this article, they centred on the ways MTEs apply knowledge in their practices	The study revolved round five university-based mathematics content courses for preservice teachers. There were four MTEs on these programmes. The project focused on the three MTEs' pedagogical interactions with their trainee teachers, especially on developing specialised content knowledge. The researchers developed two maps from the artifact database: task map (from enacted lesson plans and powerpoint slides, and classroom event map (from classroom video recordings of activities and discussions). Codes were ascertained from the analysis of the datasets concerning the development of specialised content knowledge and related MTEs pedagogical approaches. The rationale for such analysis was to understand how MTEs drew on their knowledge in their teaching activities with various groups of preservice teachers	The findings offered three knowledge types different from K-12 teachers' know-how. These were knowledge of concepts relating to preservice teachers' mathematics learning (e.g., student errors, multiplication algorithms and place value). The second type was the knowledge linking the theory to practice (e.g., connecting student errors to pedagogical approaches), relating algorithms to the K-6 curriculum, and the third one, connecting research to mathematics content learning Arising from the findings were two themes: unpacking knowledge used by MTEs, and process for identifying knowledge base for teacher education. Regarding the first theme that focused on the three knowledge types, the authors suggested mathematical knowledge required for teaching teachers was different from teachers' knowledge to teach students. The educators needed to know preservice teachers' specialised content knowledge, learning approaches of preservice teachers to teach mathematics and able to facilitate preservice teachers' recognition of these connections Concerning the second theme, the authors offered some insights. These included MTEs reflections before nd after their delivery. This approach might enable MTEs to ascertain potential mathematical and pedagogical/ instructional interactions, identify tacit knowledge forms in observing teaching, and examine the connections between the MTEs lesson plans and their implementation

(continued)

Methodological Approach 109

Table 5.1 (continued)

Author, year and title	Description of the study	Theoretical underpinnings	Methodology	Significant findings
48. Swart et al. (2018) Teacher educators' personal practical knowledge of language	This article from researchers in the Netherlands studies teacher educators' understanding of communication in higher education teaching. The paper seeks to support knowledge construction using teacher educators' perspectives of personal practical knowledge of language. It uses data from focus group interviews with 35 teacher educators. The findings indicated an emerging theorisation of two language modalities of personal practical knowledge: 'language-sensitive and interpersonally oriented' and 'language-focused and pedagogically oriented'	The theoretical frameworks revolved around the idea that language was the main source for making meaning and its development was dependent on practical experiences in social interactions (DiCerbo et al. 2014). Researcher such as Clandinin (1985), Darling-Hammond (2006) focused on personal practical knowledge as an approach to consider past and future experiences in teaching. Others (e.g., Schleppegell and O'Hallaron 2011) used language to study classroom communication as part of a teacher's personal practical knowledge. This study investigates the teacher educators' personal practical knowledge of language	The study involved 35 teacher educators in 7 teacher training institutes of Universities of Applied Sciences in the Netherlands. The first phase focused on these educators' professional development of language and communications, where personal theory of classroom practice was used. This theory consisted of the participants' practical knowledge, pedagogical and subject knowledge. Using purposive sampling, participants from seven departments took part over two years. In the focus group interviews, data of four aspects were collected. They included experiences of recent language communication, their levels, perceptions and preferences, views of meaning and relevance concerning their personal practical knowledge, and preferences for developing this language knowledge. The data was transcribed and analyses	The findings found three themes. There were (1) meaning of personal practical knowledge of language, (2) relevance of this know-how, and 3. improving this know-how for classroom communication
The first theme created 22 types (e.g., professional development, interactive practice with colleagues, time availability and collaborative practices) with four key categories: teaching, professional development, insight, and reflection and awareness. 'Meaning' might be viewed as 'undergoing the experience of teaching' and 'being a teacher' (p. 173)
The second theme generated 15 categories, and the most frequent ones were being attentive to language during teaching, language development being part of learning development and vice versa, interactive practice with learners, and interactive practice with colleagues
The third theme offered 26 categories and the four most frequent ones included language-oriented training and development, interactive practices with colleagues, more time, and working collaboratively
The researchers suggested that student learning in classrooms was dependent on the quality of teacher educators' use of language, and their awareness of personal practical knowledge of language. Resulting from this project, the researchers suggested that personal practical knowledge of language was based on past experiences (and not current awareness or future anticipation). Emerging from these findings were two theories of personal practical knowledge of language. They were 'language-sensitive and interpersonally oriented' and 'language-focused and pedagogically oriented'

(continued)

Table 5.1 (continued)

Author, year and title	Description of the study	Theoretical underpinnings	Methodology	Significant findings
49. Thinzarkyaw (2020) The Practice of Technological Pedagogical Content Knowledge of Teacher Educators in Education Colleges in Myanmar	This study focused on the application of technological pedagogical content knowledge (TPACK) of teacher educators in Myanmar. A questionnaire was used. Its findings ascertained that there were no significant differences in the TPACK practices of these educators regarding the teaching institutions, experiences, qualifications, job roles, disciplines and gender. However, there were significant differences concerning other factors	The project used Mishra and Koehler's (2006) TPACK conceptual framework comprising of knowledge, content, pedagogy, and technology. Knowledge consisted of seven types. They are technological knowledge (TK) (knowledge about technologies involving operational skills), pedagogical knowledge (PK) (knowledge of strategies, teaching principles, classroom management and organisation), content knowledge (CK) (knowledge of a specific content area), pedagogical content knowledge (PCK) (knowledge of content and pedagogy), technological content knowledge (TCK) (knowledge of technologies and their uses in teaching), technological pedagogic knowledge (TPK) (knowledge of teaching strategies to technologies), and technological pedagogical content knowledge (TPCK) (teachers' knowledge for guiding their students' learning)	The two research questions were: 1. What are the practices of teacher educators' technological pedagogical content knowledge in Education Colleges in Myanmar? 2. Do the practices of teacher educators' technological pedagogical content knowledge vary with respect to their (1) Education College (2) teaching experience (3) degree (4) rank (5) department, and (6) gender? (p. 162) The study used a survey to collect data pertaining to 108 teacher educators in three education colleges in Myanmar. It has the following categories: education colleges, gender, teaching experiences, academic qualifications, teaching roles and department (academic or education). The first part of the survey related to demographics as listed above as categories. The second part comprised of survey questions on the types of knowledge as indicated in the theoretical column. The data was collected, analysed, and recorded in tabular format	A finding from this project indicated that the level of application of the teacher educators' technological pedagogical content knowledge (TPACK) was not significant across the education colleges. Also, the teacher educators' varying teaching experiences, academic qualifications or job roles made no difference to applying TPCK in their teaching. However, when comparing the means of these educators' TPACK, the findings indicated that their application levels were higher for CK, PK and PCK than TK, TCK, TPK and TPCK. Teacher educators with higher educational levels applied TPACK more than those with lower academic qualifications. Young educators used more TK than older ones The researchers suggested that teacher educators with lower TRACK level might be due to the lack of supportive infrastructure, especially accessing technology

(continued)

Table 5.1 (continued)

Author, year and title	Description of the study	Theoretical underpinnings	Methodology	Significant findings
50. Wu and Cai (2022) Does school teaching experience matter in teaching prospective secondary mathematics teachers? Perspectives of university mathematics teacher educators	In this China-based project, the authors posed the questions: do mathematics teacher educators require school teaching experiences, and if so, how do these experiences contribute to their teaching? In this qualitative study, university-based Chinese mathematics teacher educators were interviewed regarding the two research questions. The findings testified to the importance of school teaching experiences, where various factors were identified	The three theoretical components were: teaching experience, teaching versus teaching how to teach, and school teaching experience and teacher educators' teaching practice Teaching experience might be viewed as process and product (Liu and Hou 2017; Xia 2014) referring to personal teaching experience, stakeholders (as process), and requiring knowledge, dispositions, skills, and reflection (as product) Regarding the second component, the authors stated that the roles of mathematics teachers are different than those of mathematics teacher educators. Leikin et al. (2018) offered teacher educators' triad involving content component of mathematical and didactical challenges, sensitivity to mathematics teachers, and management of teacher learning The third component focused on school teaching experience and teacher educators' teaching practice. Williams (2014) argued that MTEs' prior school teaching experiences added to their teaching practice. Male (2005) found that despite prior teaching experiences, novice teacher educators took 2–3 years to establish their new occupational identities	Ten mathematics teacher educators in Chinese universities were initially surveyed with follow-up with semi-structured interviews. The participants had varying experiences regarding their school-based mathematics teaching experiences, diversity of backgrounds, and types of universities. The interview questions focused on the roles of school teaching mathematical pedagogical programmes of mathematics teaching and the participants' perspectives of the applicability of school teaching experiences in addressing mathematics teaching. The data was transcribed and analysed. The findings on school teaching experiences included knowledge, competency, and dispositions. The findings concerning their interpretation of school teaching included nature, renewal, growth and transcendence. For those without school experiences excluded nature of school-based experiences	The exploratory study, five teacher educators had school mathematics teaching experiences, and the other five had no prior school teaching experiences. Both groups agreed that school teaching experience was imperative especially regarding knowledge, competency, and disposition for teaching mathematics. Knowledge might include school mathematics, knowledge of students' mathematical thinking and learning, knowledge of well-developed teaching approaches, capability to model school delivery, and confidence to teach mathematics teaching (as teacher educators). The project suggested that school mathematics teaching experiences was necessary. However, this was not sufficient on its own for teaching mathematics teaching. The participants offered three types of teaching models/cases based on implementation, observation and reading The participants also suggested that those with school teaching experiences needed renewal, growth and links with educational concepts and research. Those with and without teaching based experiences would have different process and products. Those with teaching-based and non-teaching-based experiences connected two approaches regarding teaching cases: 'conceptually plus operationally' and 'conceptually'. Those educators without prior school experiences could only describe and illustrate teaching cases in teaching how to teach. Those with school experiences went further to implement the teaching cases Teaching-based experiences apparently offer mathematics teacher educators a "bidirectional link between educational theory and teaching practice" (p. 675)

(continued)

Table 5.1 (continued)

Author, year and title	Description of the study	Theoretical underpinnings	Methodology	Significant findings
51. Zazkis and Mamolo (2018) From disturbance to task design, or a story of a rectangular lake	This Canadian publication investigates a teacher educator's response to a teaching incident, which utilises her personal mathematical knowledge and experiences	Focus and research on teacher educators became prominent in the latter part of the first decade of the twenty-first century, with two developments by Jaworski and Wood (2008)—International Handbook of Mathematics Teacher Education—and the start of the journal—Mathematics Teacher Educator—in 2012. The emphasis on mathematical knowledge gained traction in the publications by Zazkis and Leikin (2010), Watson and Chick (2013), and Beswick et al. (2014). The theoretical frameworks espoused in this article centred on teacher educator's personal mathematics knowledge in connection with "levels of awareness" (Mason 1998), concept of contingency (Rowland 2005), and 'knowledge at the mathematical horizon" (Zazkis and Mamolo 2011) Mason (1998) offered three types of awareness: awareness-in-action (ability to act in the moment), awareness-in-discipline (ability to articulate awareness-in-action to others), and awareness-in-counsel (sensitivity to "what others require for building or enhancing their awareness") (p. 503) Zazkis and Mamolo (2011) centred on a teacher's application of mathematical subject matter knowledge over and beyond the compulsory school curriculum and teaching. They applied Husserl's philosophical concept of horizon to include a person's focus on an object. For these two authors, a teacher's horizon knowledge relates to "an awareness of a mathematical object's periphery and can be characterised by a flexibility in focus of attention such that relevant properties, generalities, or connections, which embed the object within a greater mathematical structure, are accessed in teaching situations" (p. 504). To this end, Zazkis and Mamolo (2011) argued that teachers' Advanced Mathematical Knowledge (AMK) offered a higher and wider perspective of the horizon	The article focused on a teacher educator's pedagogic experiences based on Mason's (2002) theories of 'account-of' (elements of the story) and 'accounting-for' (from the narrative elements, analysis relating to explanations, interpretation and value judgment were elucidated). The teacher educator's experiences were based on the two authors' real teaching experiences (as exemplified by Clandinin and Connelly's (2000) narrative inquiry methodological approach	The discussion section provided the background and context of 'Naomi' to the discussion. There were two tasks. The first covered a calculation of area of a lake. The second one was a follow-up problem and solution in a narrative format The discussion focused on the scripts produced by teachers on why Alex's solution resulted in a correct answer. Three themes included 'accounting for', 'contingency', and 'awareness, contingency and horizon' The first theme—accounting for—appeared in two guises: Naomi as a mathematics teacher and a teacher educator. As a mathematics teacher Naomi's personal mathematical knowledge gave her a deeper appreciation of the discipline (mathematics) and a wider perspective of the content and its applicability to students' learning, thus extending her understanding of awareness-in-discipline and awareness-in-counsel as a teacher educator. As a teacher educator Naomi's use of scripting task created opportunities to develop her awareness-in-counsel. The scripting task also enabled teachers to appreciate different and relevant mathematical connections across the mathematics curriculum, a sense of what details or depth are relevant in the classroom, and a 'student-appropriate' explanation might inform a 'colleague-appropriate' one. The last point referred to not losing sight of the challenging mathematics theory The contingency theme referred to Naomi's responses to her students' 'awareness-in'. This contingency experience in the script writing task enabled Naomi to focus on class discussion and, thus, widened her perspective of developing and fostering teachers' KML With the third theme (covering awareness, contingency and horizon), the authors identified another discipline (compared to Mason's mathematics discipline): mathematics-teaching. The new discipline related to a teacher educator's awareness-in-counsel, which was also the teacher educator's awareness-in-discipline of mathematics-teaching. The authors describe it as the "awareness results in developing of mathematically salient scenarios that could provoke a moment of disturbance for prospective teachers" (p. 514) The teacher's horizon knowledge might be typologized into inner horizon (features of the object) and outer horizon (such as disciplinary ideas, practices and structural component that contextualise the specific teaching situation)

Methodological Approach 113

Table 5.1 (continued)

Author, year and title	Description of the study	Theoretical underpinnings	Methodology	Significant findings
52. Zazkis and Zazkis (2011) The significance of mathematical knowledge in teaching elementary methods courses: perspective of mathematics teacher educators	This Canadian-US article studies mathematics teacher educators' application of their mathematical knowledge in teaching 'Methods of Teaching Elementary Mathematics' programmes. Using interviews, five experienced primary school mathematics teachers elucidated their perspectives with two emerging themes	The literature sources focused on two themes: the practice of mathematics teacher educators and teachers' knowledge and awareness. In the first theme, Zaslavsky (2008) argued that teacher educators are 'self-made' and used their experiences as mathematics deliverers, whereas Chapman (2008) suggested that instructional approaches appeared to assist the teachers in their work. Disciplinary knowledge was required. However, teaching mathematics knowledge was perceived to be complicated where factors such as pedagogy, psychology, didactics, research, theories, curriculum, and mathematics were involved The second theme centred on teachers' knowledge and awareness. Types of teachers' knowledge were discussed, including subject matter knowledge, pedagogical content knowledge, common content knowledge, and specialised content knowledge. Davis and Simmt (2006) avoided the separation of content and pedagogy, and Watson (2008) dispensed with categorisation as unhelpful as it might disguised the "essential mathematics activity in which different kinds of knowledge relate and inform each other" (p. 249). Mason (1998) saw 'levels of awareness' as a feature of teachers' knowledge with two types. Awareness-in-action (ability to correct a mistake and suggest an answer) is the first type, and awareness-in-discipline (ability to instruct others to correct mistake and provide solution) is the second type	Five experienced primary/elementary school mathematics teachers participated in this survey using interviews. They were asked about the value of their mathematical knowledge regarding teaching of an elementary mathematics methods programme and whether there were opportunities to apply their own disciplinary knowledge	After analysing the five mathematics teacher educators' perspectives, two themes emerged. They were different mathematics and task design The teacher educators acknowledged the various mathematics knowledge. Watson (2008) suggested disciplinary mathematics and school mathematics were taught under the same name, 'mathematics'. This project found that when these educators discussed their mathematical applications to their learners, concepts and approaches consistent with disciplinary mathematics The other theme on task design, the authors argued that school mathematics is not a subset of disciplinary mathematics, but as intersection between the two sets. Thus, task design was viewed as a conduit for implementing teachers' mathematical knowledge

8. Further analysis and synthesis were carried out from the two sources—Table 5.1 and notes—focusing on the two research questions. Trends from this process were ascertained and included in the next section.

The steps, mentioned above, provided this study with the following methodological approaches employed by the final list of publications in Table 5.1. These approaches covered funding sources, research methods (quantitative and qualitative), and research sites.

Interestingly, there is no apparent systematic review of literature on teacher educator knowledge carried out to date. Thus, this systematic review of literature on the topic appears to be the first.

Findings and Discussion

This lengthy section consists of two parts: the first relates to the analysis of the 52 identified literature sources on teacher educator knowledge, and the second answers the two research questions identified earlier.

Part 1—Analysis of the 52 Literature Sources

The first part is divided into the following sections: descriptions of the chosen publications, the use of relevant literature sources, methodological approaches, and findings and discussions. These sections relate to Table 5.1 columns. The 52 chosen publications ranged from 2000 to 2023. If these publications were divided into the periods of 2000–2005, 2006–2010, 2011–2015, 2016–2020 and 2021–2023, then the number of publications would be 2, 9, 9, 16 and 16 respectively. The trends indicate the increasing publications in the latter years after a slow start in the first period of 2000–2005. Interestingly, the final period of 2021–2023, only three years, yielded the most numbers of relevant publications per year.

Descriptions of the Chosen Publications

In this column, there will be three descriptions of the publications. The first relates to the country of publication (based on the authors and/or project location), second refers to the nature/topic of the study, and third educational discipline.

Regarding the single-based country of publication, the most publications came from the US at 13 out of the 52 publications. The second highest number from a single country was Australia—10. England has five, Canada 3, and the Netherlands, Norway, and Spain 2. The rest of these countries had one publication each: Argentina, China, Denmark, Finland, Hong Kong, India, Indonesia, Israel, Ireland,

Findings and Discussion 115

Myanmar, Thailand, and Turkey. Of the four publications from various countries, one set was from Asia (Bhutan, Malaysia, and Pakistan) and Europe (Denmark, Estonia, and France) (No. 17), another from English-speaking countries (Australia, Canada, England, and the US) (No. 35), the Netherlands and China (No. 44), and North America (Canada and the US) (No. 52).

Concerning the nature of study, knowledge-related publications with the highest frequency totalled 40. Practice and pedagogy topic had 17 mentions, professional development, 5, curriculum and skills, 2. The other education-related areas of coherent education, commercialization, craft, digitalization, equity and justice, feminism, gender, identity, physical education, race, resources, and routes/pathways had one mention each. Please note that a publication may have more than one area.

Referring to the education disciplines or subjects, mathematics features the most with 12 mentions, higher education 8, science and colleges each with 5, primary 4, compulsory and secondary education each with 3, English and Biology with 2, and Physical education, Chemistry, EFL, literacy and technology 1.

Use of Relevant Literature Sources

The theoretical underpinnings of the 52 publications consisted of four main areas. These included knowledge, pedagogies, professional development, and miscellaneous. Knowledge (as indicated in the previous section on 'description of the study') also featured the most in the literature review column—40 occurrences. Shulman's (1987) 'pedagogical content knowledge' was referenced in eight publications (Nos. 1, 4, 11, 20, 21, 24, 28 and 33). Technological pedagogical content knowledge (TPACK) had five mentions in publications 16, 17, 36, 40, and 49. Teaching learning model (Cochran-Smith and Lyte 1999) featured three times in publications 25, 42, and 47. Clandinin's (1985) 'personal practical knowledge' was mentioned in publications 28 and 48. Other knowledge forms related to technology, content knowledge, science teacher educators' knowledge, professional practical knowledge, etc.

Pedagogies (with 17 mentions) covered triad of mathematical pedagogies, critical pedagogy, feminist theory, critical race theory, model of integrated pedagogies for professional expertise, etc. Professional development (with 5 mentions) propounded by Murray (2005), Knight et al. (2014), Boyd and Harris (2010) and Flores (2018) were some of the pertinent sources mentioned in the publications review of literature. Other theoretical underpinnings included tensions, awareness, social theory of reflexivity, model of subjectivity relating to curriculum, tacit aspects, model of interdependent constructions, coherence, and identities. The related literature sources are in Table 5.1.

Methodological Approaches

The methodological approaches and research methods used by the 52 publications were varied. The most frequently used research method was interview, which appeared in 20 publications. The next was questionnaires/survey in 13 publications, documentary research with 10, observations 8, self-study 6, vignettes of experiential experiences 5, phenomenological study 4, social laboratories, 3, and autobiography, journals, and hypothetical case studies, 1. The projects might use more than one data collection method especially in the phenomenological studies.

Findings and Discussion

The findings/discussions from the 52 publications are varied in their complexities of their chosen researched areas. However, two types may be identified. They are typology and impact. The first—typology—refers to identification of typologies, taxonomies or themes resulting from the analysis of the empirical data. This type can be scheme of classification or topic for discussion resulting from a research study/ project. Impact relates to effect or influence findings on a setting/situation or stakeholders. Effect or influence use in this context may also include understanding the phenomenon in an educational setting. These explanations from literary definitions offer a deeper approach to discussing this section.

Within the first type—typology—there are variations. They cover five learner roles of teacher educators (no. 1), four themes of teacher educators' professional development (no. 3), taxonomy of ELT and language teacher educator knowledge types (no. 5), typology of three types of personal emergent properties (no. 12), and three types of learning for teacher educators (reflection-in-action, syntactic teaching structures and listening to candidates) (no. 15). Also, there are four professional development themes for Chemistry teacher educators (no. 16), four themes of teacher educators' professional development in virtual learning spaces (no. 18), four aspects of content knowledge of Mathematics teacher educators' development (no. 19), five knowledge domains of teacher educators (no. 26), and six knowledge types on open education resources for teacher educators (no. 29), two main categories (academic and professional) of teacher educators' characteristics with sub-categories (no. 30), and five types of practical professional knowledge of teacher educators (no. 31). Furthermore, this first type includes five spectra of Confucian teacher educators (no. 33), typology of four narrative themes of craft and teacher educators (no. 34), four themes on research, pedagogy of higher education, literacy and teaching of teacher educators (no. 35), thematic findings of FE teacher educators on teacher education, becoming FE teacher educators, knowledge, identities and professional development (no. 37), four areas of teacher educators' knowledge of practice (no. 38), four knowledge domains of science teacher educators (no. 39), seven themes of digital competences in teacher educators' knowledge (no. 40), three themes on race (family histories, scholarly experiences and embodiment) of teacher educators' beliefs and teaching (no. 41), 31 knowledge sources of Mathematics teacher educators (no. 42), typology of teacher educators' pedagogical content knowledge (no. 43), three themes of teacher educators' practices (no. 44), typology of teacher educators' content-specific, general pedagogical and content knowledge (no. 45), four teacher educators' knowledge types (no. 46), three knowledge types of K-12

Mathematics teacher educators (no. 47), and three categories (and sub-categories) of communication of teacher educators' personal practical knowledge of language (no. 48).

The second type—impact—covers Mathematics teacher educators' opportunities for developing trainee teachers' knowledge (no. 2), teacher educators' perspectives of content knowledge of physical education (no. 4), construction of knowledge development of a teacher educator's personal development of knowledge and teaching (no. 6), tensions of teacher educators in professional practice (no. 7), sacred stories as professional learning and resistance (no. 8), teacher educators' identity and knowledge growth (no. 9), necessity of pedagogical content knowledge in geography education (no. 11), commodification of subject knowledge towards teacher educators' mentoring role rather than educational role (no. 13), and importance of 'basis-for-knowing' of teacher educators (no. 14). Similarly, the topics include professional development of teacher educators using Mishra and Koehler's (2006) TPACK model (no. 17), development of SMTPACK model (no. 20), impact of critical experiences on science teacher educators (no. 21), race as an integral to RPCK in social studies (no. 22), impact of coherence in teacher educators on policy etc., (no. 23), limitations of teacher educators' PCK in teaching science teaching (no. 24), greater professional development of teacher educators linking knowledge-in-teaching and knowledge-of-practice (no. 25), teacher educators' actions and their connections with personal practical knowledge (no. 27), relevance of subject-specific pedagogy knowledge in post-compulsory teacher educators (no. 28), and EFL teacher educators' professional development of their SMK, PK, OGS and SAS (no. 32). The other topics cover differences of gender and taught subjects, and technological knowledge types of teacher educators in education colleges (no. 36), understanding of TPACK of teacher educators (no. 49), impact of school teaching experiences on Mathematics teacher educators (no. 50), understanding of teacher educators of the three awareness types (awareness-in-action, awareness-in-discipline, and awareness-in-counsel) (no. 51), and understanding of Mathematics teacher educators' different mathematics and task design (no. 52).

To summarise Part 1, it covers the analysis of the 52 literature sources. This analysis has four sub-headings: description of the studies, theoretical underpinnings, methodology and significant findings. With the descriptions, country-based publications were identified. The country with most publications was the US. The other lesser-known countries included Argentina, Indonesia, Myanmar, and Thailand. There were also four publications covering more than one country. The most frequently researched topic was knowledge, with 40 mentions, followed by practice and pedagogy, with 17 occurrences. Concerning the education disciplines, Mathematics came top with 12 mentions, followed by higher education with 8. Theoretical underpinnings column was focused on knowledge-related projects with 40 mentions and pedagogies with 17. The two most popular research methods were interviews and questionnaires. The findings/discussions from the 52 publications were divided into two types—typology and impact—with wide variations of researched topics from the

52 publications. The analysis of the publications provided a rich and complex array of descriptions, theoretical frameworks, methodologies, and findings/discussions of teacher educators' knowledge.

Part 2—Answering the Two Research Questions

In the second part, the two research questions refer to the extent of occupational education and overlaps between the education sectors in the 52 literature sources.

Extent of Vocationalism

Of the 52 chosen relevant publications in Table 5.1, five (or 10%) were allocated to (further education) colleges. They are nos. 23, 28, 34, 37, and 49. As 73.2% of the teachers/lecturers in FE colleges in England deliver occupational programmes (Frontier Economics 2020, Fig. 54), it is pertinent and relevant to focus on occupational/ vocational aspects of teacher educators (as indicated in the first research question in this chapter).

This section aims to answer the research question by describing the five related publications and discussing their relevance to occupational education. Their relevance covers the topics, literature sources and impact occupational/vocational study in general.

Duch and Nielsen (2022) (no. 23) centered on how vocational teacher educators in Denmark balance the different perspectives and support coherence among vocational teachers. Using three published qualitative empirical studies on policy documents, one-to-one interviews, focus group interviews and observations, they studied the teacher educators' coherence in their teacher education courses and challenges and tensions.

Hanley and Thompson (2021) (no. 28) studied the preparation of teacher educators in the English FE sector. The study used an interventionist methodological approach of workshops on 36 teacher educators. These workshops included mini-lectures, group activities, resources, questionnaire, and telephone interviews. The intention was to understand subject-specialist pedagogy using a socially constructed pedagogical content knowledge (PCK) approach.

Kidd et al. (2022) (no. 34) explored using narrative of two English vocational teacher educators how they facilitated their teacher trainees' development using craft as a theoretical framework. The study also studied the educators' professional development. The investigated used reflectivity to conceptualise this double hermeneutic (i.e., the craft of teacher educators and craft of trainee teachers). In so doing, it raised issues regarding know-how and two boundary crossings. The first crossing relates to FE trainees moving from their VET settings to training to teach their specialist subjects. The second refers to teacher educators transferring from delivering VET in FE colleges to teacher education courses based in universities.

Findings and Discussion   119

Loo (2020) (no. 37) published the first research monograph on English FE teacher educators. The relevant chapters included Chap. 2 on teacher education, C4, routes and pathways to be teacher educators, C5 teacher educators' knowledge, C6 professional identities, and C7 their professional development/education. Based on 33 teacher educators from the FE colleges, universities and private providers in England, the empirical data relied on a questionnaire, face-to-face interviews, supporting documents, and Talking Heads (an unstructured form of interviews that participants had ownership).

This final publication by Thinzarkyaw (2020) (no. 49) was carried out in Myanmar. It focused on college teacher educators' technological pedagogical content knowledge (TPACK) using a quantitative research method (questionnaire) of 108 teacher educators from three education colleges. It centered on knowledge types (hence TPACK), gender, teaching experiences, academic qualifications, teaching roles, and institutional departments.

This section is divided into the topics, literature sources and impact occupational/vocational study in general. Duch and Nielsen (2022) studied the educators' coherence, the teacher education courses, and challenges and tensions within those settings. Hanley and Thompson (2021) focused on teacher educators and their understanding of subject-specialist (including occupation-related areas such as engineering, manufacturing, and hair and beauty) pedagogy within a social setting. Kidd et al. (2022) ascertained the boundary crossings of vocational teacher educators from college to university. Loo (2020) covered broader spectrum of teacher educators from pathways/routes, knowledge, identities, and professional development. Thinzarkyaw (2020) studied college teachers' TPACK, though not specifically on vocational related subjects, thus discounting its relevance to this chapter.

The salient literature sources/concepts used by the five publications included Hammerness (2006) and Heggen and Smeby (2012) on coherence education (no. 23), Bernstein (1996) and Shulman (1987) on pedagogy (no. 28), and Sennett (2006) on craft (no. 34). For publication no. 37, the pertinent sources were Becher (1994), Evans (2016), Loo (2018), Kemmis and Green (2013), Kahneman (2012), Gee (2000, 2001), Boyd and Harris (2010), Murray (2005), Knight et al. (2014) on pathways, knowledge, identities and professional development, and no. 49, Mishra and Koehler (2006) on TPACK.

Regarding impact on work-related study, Duch and Nielsen's (2022) (no. 23) study offers another perspective to explore issues and tensions by vocational teacher educators in their complex roles. The coherence framework is novel to this work-related area. Hanley and Thompson's (2021) (no. 28) study provides a timespan of teacher educators' issues surrounding subject-specialism teacher education. The findings from this study are needed to critique and start a dialogue about the conventional generic pedagogical approach to teacher education in the sector. This study is relevant as one of the significant roles of teacher educators relate to educating trainee teachers. Kidd et al. (2022) (no. 34) use craft as a conceptual framework to understand vocational teacher educators' boundary crossing perspectives. These perspectives are salient to these educators in the FE community. Loo (2020) (no.

37) offers a broad and empirically focused monograph on vocational teacher educators. The breadth of areas covered provides an essential reference to those interested in this work-related area that is lamentably under-researched. Thinzarkyaw's study (2020) (no. 49) does not explicitly include vocational areas, but it covers colleges and technological know-how, which will have relevance to this technologically based society.

Overlaps Between Education Sectors

This section covers the relevance of the occupational/vocational publications in the FE sector to the other ones, commonalities and differences, and relevance of the vocational literature sources for studies to the other sectors.

FE education sector is viewed as a poor cousin to the other sectors of compulsory education (primary and secondary), higher and professional education. FE sector's characteristics (i.e., porosity, inclusivity, diversity, and occupational courses) were discussed in Chap. 1.

The obvious common aspect revolves teacher educators. The topics from the vocational publications, such as boundary-crossing, subject-specialism delivery, issues and tensions, knowledge (including TPACK), identities, and professional development, are also studied by researchers in other education sectors, exemplified in Table 5.1. Take the example of teacher educators' knowledge, this topic was studied by no. 37 in FE and 39 publications (nos. 1–8, 10–22, 24, 27, 29–32, 35–36, 39, 40, 42–43, 45, 47–49, and 51–52). Theoretical frameworks (e.g., Shulman 1987) used by the vocational publications covered in the previous section were also used by other publications. Shulman's typology could be found in non-occupational publications nos. 1, 4, 11, 20, 21, 24, 28, and 33, totalling eight that were specific to pedagogical content knowledge (PCK). One may also include variations of Shulman's knowledge typology, such as TPACK (nos. 16, 17, 36, and 40) and content knowledge (no. 19).

Differences between FE and the other sectors include the obvious area of occupational/vocational education. Concepts including craft (Sennett 2006) (no. 34) would be specific to vocational studies. The other difference is subject specificity, where in vocational areas may include engineering, and health and beauty. In the compulsory and higher education sectors, subjects may cover science, Mathematics, English, etc.

Concerning relevance of vocational/occupational to other education sectors, the answer is the previous section (in answer to question 1).

To summarise Part 2, it delineated the two research questions on vocationalism and overlaps with other education sectors. These discussions covered descriptions of the relevant publications, their relevance to vocational education, and commonalities and differences to other sectors.

Conclusion

This systematic review of literature chapter on teacher educators' knowledge covered related literature from 2000 to 2023 totalling 52 publications (Table 5.1). The findings/discussion section delineated the analysis of the publications and the two research questions indicated at the start of the chapter. This extended chapter will, hopefully, provide a significant platform for discussions on occupational/vocational teacher educators' knowledge.

References[1]

Abell SK, Park Rogers MA, Hanusein DL, Lee MH, Gagnon MJ (2009) Preparing the next generation of science teacher educators: a model for developing PCK for teaching science teachers. J Sci Teacher Educ 20(1):77–93

Appova A, Taylor CE (2019) Expert mathematics teacher educators' purposes and practices for providing prospective teachers with opportunities to develop pedagogical content knowledge in content courses. J Math Teacher Educ 22:179–204

Ariza RP, del Pozo RM, Toscano JM (2002) Conceptions of school-based teacher educators concerning ongoing teacher education. Teach Teach Educ 18:305–321

Backman E, Pearson P, Forrest GJ (2019) The value of movement content knowledge in the training of Australian PE teachers: perceptions of teacher educators. Curriculum Stud. Health Phys. Educ. 10(2):187–203

Banegas DL (2022) Teacher educators' funds of knowledge for the preparation of future teachers. RELC J 53(3):686–702

Bates T, Swennen A (2012) Professional development of teacher educators. Routledge, Abingdon

Becher T (1994) The significance of disciplinary differences. Stud High Educ 19:151–161. https://doi.org/10.1080/03075079412331382007

Bernstein B (1996) Pedagogy, symbolic control and identity: theory, research, critique. London, Taylor and Francis Limited

Berry A (2007) Reconceptualizing teacher educator knowledge as tensions: exploring the tension between valuing and reconstructing experiences. Stud Teach Educ 3(2):117–134

Berry A (2008) Tensions in teaching about teaching: understanding practice as a teacher educator. Springer, Cham

Berry A (2009) Professional self-understanding as expertise in teaching about teaching. Teach Teach Theory Pract 15(2):305–318

Berry A, Forgasz (2018) Disseminating secret-story-knowledge through the self-study of teacher education practices. Stud Teach Educ 14(3):235–245

Berry A, Scheele S (2007) Professional learning together: building teacher educator knowledge through collaborative research

Beswick K, Goos M (2018) Mathematics teacher educator knowledge: what do we know and where to from here? J Math Teacher Educ 21:417–427

Blankman M, van der Schee J, Volman M, Boogaard M (2015) Primary teacher educators' perception of desired and achieved pedagogical content knowledge in geography education in primary teacher training. Int Res Geogr Environ Educ 24(1):80–94

Boland A, Cherry MG, Dickson R (eds) (2017) Doing a systematic review: a student's guide. Sage, London

---

[1] Please note references listed in Table 5.1 are not included due to word count constraint.

Bourke T, Ryan M, Rowan L, Brownless JL, Walker S, L'Estrange L (2023) Teacher educators' knowledge about diversity: what enables and constrains their teaching decisions? Asia-Pac J Teach Educ 51(1):28–44

Boyd P, Harris K (2010) Becoming a university lecturer in teacher education: expert school teachers reconstructing their pedagogy and identity. Prof Dev Educ 36(1):9–24

Brown T, Rowley H, Smith K (2016) Sliding subject positions: knowledge and teacher educators. Br Edu Res J 42(3):492–507

Bullock SM (2009a) Becoming a teacher educator: the self as a basis-for-knowing. In: Counterpoints, vol 357. Making connections: self-study & social action. Peter Lang AG, pp 269–283

Bullock SM (2009b) Learning to think like a teacher educator: making the substantive and syntactic structures of teaching explicit through self-study. Teach Teach Theory Pract 15(2):291–304

Carpendale J, Delaney S, Rochette E (2020) Modelling meaningful chemistry teacher education online: reflections from chemistry preservice teacher educators in Australia. J Chem Educ 97:2534–2543

Castera J, Marre CC, Chan MKY, Sherab K, Impedovo MA, Sarapuu T, Pedregosa AD, Malik SK, Amand H (2019) Self-reported TPACK of teacher educators across six countries in Asia and Europe. Educ Inf Technol 25:3003–3019

Ceallaigh TJO (2022) Designing, navigating and nurturing virtual learning spaces: teacher educators' professional development priorities and potential pathways. Teach Teach Educ 115:103697

Chauvot JB (2008) Curricular knowledge and the work of mathematics teacher educators. Issues Teach Educ 17(2):83–99

Chick H, Beswick K (2018) Teaching teachers to teach Boris: a framework for mathematics teacher educator pedagogical content knowledge. J Math Teacher Educ 21:475–499

Clandinin J (1985) Personal practical knowledge: a study of teachers' classroom images. Curriculum Inquiry, 15(4):361–385

Cochran-Smith M, Lytle S (1999) Relationships of knowledge and practice: teacher learning in communities. In: Griffin G (ed) Rev Res Educ 24, 249–305. Washington DC, American Educational Research Association

Cooper R (2013) Using critical experiences to build understanding of science teacher educators' pedagogical knowledge. Teach Educ Pract 26(4):637–650

Crawley J (2016) Post compulsory teacher educators: connecting professionals. Critical Publishing, St. Albans, Hertfordshire

Czerniawski G (2018) Teacher educators in the 21st century: identity, knowledge and research. Critical Publishing, Albans, Hertfordshire

Davey R (2013) Professional identity of teacher educators. Routledge, Abingdon

Demoiny SB (2018) Social studies teacher educators who do race work. Soc Stud Res Pract 13(3):330–344

Department for Business, Innovation and Skills (BIS) (2012) [The Lingfield Report] Professionalism in further education: final report of the independent review panel. HMSO, London

Department for Education (DEF) (2010) The importance of teaching. The Stationery Office, London

Duch H, Nielsen BL (2022) Stakeholder perspectives on vocational teacher education and teacher educators role in supporting coherence. In: Loo S (ed) Teacher educators in vocational and further education. Springer, Cham, Switzerland

Evans K (2016) Higher vocational learning and knowledgeable practice: the newly qualified practitioner at work. In: Loo S, Jameson J (eds) Vocationalism in further and higher education: policy, programmes and pedagogy. Routledge, Abingdon

Faikhamta C, Clarke A (2013) Self-study of a Thai teacher educator developing a better understanding of PCK for teaching about teaching science. Res Sci Educ 43:955–979

Flores M A (2018) Tensions and possibilities in teacher educators' roles and professional development. Eur J Teach Educ 41(1):1–3. https://doi.org/10.1080/02619768.2018.1402984

Foster P, Hammersley M (1998) A review of reviews: structure and function in reviews of educational research. Br Edu Res J 24:609–628

References

Frontier Economics (2020) Further education workforce data for England: analysis of the 2018–19 staff individualised (SIR) data. Education & Training Foundation, London
Gee JP (2000–2001) Identity as an analytic lens for research in education. Rev Res Educ 25:99–125
Goodwin AL, Smith L, Souto-Manning M, Cheruvu R, Tan MY, Reed R, Taveras L (2014) What should teacher educators know and be able to do? Perspectives from practicing teacher educators. J Teach Educ. https://doi.org/10.1177/0022487114535266
Goodwin AL, Kosnik C (2013) Quality teacher educators = quality teachers? Conceptualizing essential domains of knowledge for those who teach teachers. Teach Dev Int J Teach Prof Dev 17(3):334–346
Gough D (2004) Systematic research synthesis. In: Thomas G, Pring R (Eds) Evidence-based practice in education. Open University Press, Buckingham
Gough D, Oliver S, Thomas J (2017) An introduction to systematic reviews. Sage, London
Hadar LL, Brody DL (2018) Teacher educators' professional learning in communities. Routledge, Abingdon
Hamilton ML, Pinnegar S (eds) (2015) Knowledge as a teacher educator. In: Knowing, becoming, doing as teacher educators: identity, intimate scholarship, inquiry. Advances in research on teaching, vol 26. Emerald Group Publishing Limited, Bingley, pp 57–66. https://doi.org/10.1108/S1479-368720140000026006
Hammerness K (2006) From coherence in theory to coherence in practice. Teach College Rec 108(7):1241–1265
Hanley P, Thompson R (2021) 'Generic pedagogy is not enough': teacher educators and specialist pedagogy in the further education and skills sector in England. Teach Teach Educ 98:103233
Heggen K, Smeby J-C (2012) Gir mest mulig samanheng også den beste profesjonsutdanninga? Norsk Pedagogisk Tidsskrift 1:4–14
Hood N, Littlejohn A (2017) Knowledge typologies for professional learning: educators' (re)generation of knowledge when learning open educational practice. Educ Technol Res Dev 651:1583–1604
Jegstad KM, Fiskum TA, Aspfors J, Eklund G (2022) Dichotomous and multifaceted: teacher educators' understanding of professional knowledge in research-based teacher education. Scand J Educ Res 66(6):1005–1019
John PD (2002) The teacher educator's experience: case studies of practical professional knowledge. Teach Teach Educ 18:323–341
Kahneman D (2012) Thinking, fast and slow. Penguin Books, London
Karim SA (2021) Bridging the gaps between teacher educators and student teachers' perceptions about the attributes of effective teacher educators. Reg J 14(1):1–24
Katyal KR, Pang MF (2010) Paradigms, perspectives and dichotomies amongst teacher educators in Hong Kong. J Educ Teach 36(3):319–332
Kemmis RB, Green A (2013) Vocational education and training teachers' conceptions of their pedagogy. Int J Train Res 11(2):101–121. https://doi.org/10.5172/ijtr.2013.11.2.101
Kidd W, Viswarajan S, McMahon A (2022) Reflexivity for whom? The ethics of a craft identity and the know-how of supporting reflexivity on teacher education programme. In: Loo S (ed) Teacher educators in vocational and further education. Springer, Cham, Switzerland
Knight SL, Lloyd GM, Arbaugh F, Gamson D, McDonald SP, Nolan J Jr (2014) Professional development and practices of teacher educators. J Teach Educ. https://doi.org/10.1177/0022487114542220
Kosnik C, Menna L, Dharamshi P, Miyata C, Cleovoulou Y, Beck C (2015) Four spheres of knowledge required: an international study of the professional development of literacy/English teacher educators. J Educ Teach 41(1):52–77
Kumar CA (2021) Technological pedagogical content knowledge of educators of teacher education program working in colleges of education. Turk J Comput Math Educ 12(14):2291–2296
Loo S (2018) Teachers and teaching in vocational and professional education. Routledge, Abingdon
Loo S (2019) Professional identities in the further education sector: a systematic literature review. In: Loo S (ed) Further education, professional and occupational pedagogy: knowledge and experiences. Routledge, Abingdon

Loo S (2020) Professional development of teacher educators in further education. Routledge, Abingdon

Loo S (ed) (2022) Teacher educators in vocational and further education. Springer, Cham, Switzerland

Loughran J, Berry A (2005) Modelling by teacher educators. Teach Teach Educ 21:193–203

Lunenberg M, Dengerink J, Korthagen F (2014) The professional teacher educator: roles, behaviour, and professional development of teacher educators. Sense Publishers, Rotterdam

McEwen-Atkins E, Merryfield M (eds) (1996) Preparing teachers to teach global perspectives: a handbook for teacher educators. Corwin Press, Thousand Oaks, California

Mishra P, Koehler MJ (2006) Technological pedagogical content knowledge: a framework for teacher knowledge. Teach Coll Rec 108(6):1017–1054. https://doi.org/10.1111/j.1467-9620.2006.00684.x

Mork SM, Henrikson EK, Haug BS, Jorde D, Froyland M (2021) Defining knowledge domains for science teacher educators. Int J Sci Educ 43(18):3018–3034

Murray J (2005) Re-addressing the priorities: new teacher educators and induction into higher education. Eur J Teach Educ 28(1):67–85

Nagel I (2021) Digital competence in teacher education curricula: what should teacher educators know, be aware of and prepare students for? Nordic J Comp Int Educ 5(4):104–122

Ohito EO (2019) Mapping women's knowledge of antiracist teaching in the United States: a feminist phenomenological study of three antiracist women teacher educators. Teach Teach Educ 86:102892

Ozmantar MF, Agac G (2021) Mathematics teacher educators' knowledge sources in teacher education practices. Math Educ Res J 35:175–201

Pascual MM, Contreras LC (2021) The pedagogical knowledge deployed by a primary mathematics teacher educator in teaching symmetry. Mathematics 9:1241

Petticrew M, Roberts H (2006) Systematic reviews in the social sciences: a practical guide. Blackwell, Oxford

Philpott C (2014) Theories of professional learning: a critical guide for teacher educators. Critical Publishing Ltd., St. Albans, Hertfordshire

Ping C, Schellings G, Beijaard D, Ye J (2021) Teacher educators' professional learning: perceptions of Dutch and Chinese teacher educators. Asia-Pac J Teach Educ 49(3):262–281

Selmer S, Bernstein M, Bolyard J (2016) Multilayered knowledge: understanding the structure and enactment of teacher educators' specialized knowledge base. Teach Dev 20(4):437–457

Sennett R (2006) The culture of the new capitalism. Yale University Press

Shulman LS (1987) Knowledge and teaching: foundations of the new reform. Harvard Educ Rev 57(1):1–22. https://doi.org/10.17763/haer.57.1.j463w79r56455411

Stillman J, Ahmed KS, Beltramo JL, Cataneda-Flores E, Garza VG, Pyo M (2019) From the ground up: cultivating teacher educator knowledge from the situated knowledges of emerging, asset-oriented teacher educators. Asia-Pac J Teach Educ 47(3):265–285

Superfine AS, Li W (2014) Exploring the mathematical knowledge needed for teaching teachers. J Teach Educ 65(4):303–314

Swart F, de Graaff R, Onstenk J, Knezic D (2018) Teacher educators' personal practical knowledge. Teach Teach Theory Practice. https://doi.org/10.1080/13540602.2017.1368477

Thinzarkyaw W (2020) The practice of technological pedagogical content knowledge of teacher educators in education colleges in Myanmar. Contemp Educ Technol 11(2):159–176

Wu Y, Cai J (2022) School teaching experience matter in teaching prospective secondary mathematics teachers? Perspectives of university-based mathematics teacher educators. Math Educ 54:665–678

Zazkis R, Manolo A (2018) From disturbance to task design, or a story of a rectangular lake. J Math Teacher Educ 21:501–516

Zazkis R, Zazkis D (2011) The significance of mathematical knowledge in teaching elementary methods courses: perspectives of mathematics teacher educators. Educ Stud Math 76:247–263

Chapter 6
Epilogue

Abstract This final chapter serves as a summary of the above four standalone chapters. It will re-cap the salient aspects of each of them. This chapter will offer overviews of the chapters and relate to connections and implications for the further education (FE) sector. In summing up, it will provide directions for furthering the empirical findings of this monograph for the relevant stakeholders such as researchers, lecturers, FE college managers, policymakers, and networks (e.g., the Institute for Apprenticeships and Technical Education (IfATE), the Learning and Skills Research Network (LSRN), and the Teacher Education in Lifelong Learning (TELL)).

Keywords Summary · Re-cap · Implications and applications · Conclusion

Introduction

It is worth remembering, in the first chapter, "this research monograph aims to offer interested readers deep insights into how lecturers and teacher educators perform as educationists. These performative actions cover their know-how, pedagogic agencies, and identities" (Chap. 1). The amoebic social space of the further education (FE) sector in England has four characteristics: porosity, inclusivity, diversity, and work-related programmes. Social justice underpins these four characteristics. The four standalone chapters in the monograph (re-cap in the next section) need to be read with the monograph aims, and FE characteristics in mind.

This chapter has four sections. After the introduction, the following section re-caps the four chapters. The third section provides implications and applications, and the conclusion section summarises the book's findings and offers three levels (micro, meso, and macro) of areas for further research.

Re-cap of the Monograph

Chapter 2 provided a Mark II version of the conceptual framework of the occupational pedagogies of teachers (Loo 2018). The framework is applied explicitly to all occupational/vocational programmes using an epistemological approach to teacher knowledge. This knowledge is defined broadly, covering knowledge, experiences, capabilities/abilities, and skillsets. Occupational education (OE), a new education area, encompasses TEVT, higher vocational and professional education across the three academic levels of pre-university, higher and professional education. The Mark II version in this chapter clarified socio-cultural contexts, non-linearity and dynamic characteristics of the framework, defined teachers' know-how and recontextualization and the framework's complexities. It also further developed and thus highlighted the differences between occupational and academic subject pedagogies and discussed the intellectual space concerning identity formation. The third development included two knowledge applications of 'signature pedagogies' (Shulman 2005) and 'logic of practice' (Bourdieu 1992). These two applications complemented the other knowledge applications of 'knowledgeable practice' (Evans 2016), 'five complexities of occupational pedagogy' (Loo 2012), 'ongoing recontextualization' (Loo 2014), 'practice architecture' (Kemmis and Green 2013), and Systems 1 and 2 (Kahneman 2012). The Mark II version provided intellectual and practical spaces to understand and implement occupational and academic subject pedagogies and, hopefully, start a discourse between the artificial constructions of the two pedagogies. The framework highlights, importantly, the complexities of occupational pedagogy, providing a throughput approach from theoretical knowledge of the disciplines to curriculum development (i.e., knowledge acquisition) and to teaching deliveries via the choices of teaching strategies (i.e., knowledge application).

Chapter 3 was on occupational education of teacher educators' knowledge and pedagogy in teaching settings of FE colleges, universities, and private providers. It provided a deep understanding of these educators' know-how types, sources, and applications. The chapter highlighted the complexities of these educationists. Its comparison between the three teaching settings showed the commonalities of broad knowledge types, sources, experiences, attitudes, and skill sets as well as the differences. Noticeable differences included university educators having a greater sense of their requirements and awareness as a specific educational cohort for possible future studies and research and those in the private sector having a culturally international perspective of their work.

Chapter 4 examined the professional identities of English teachers and teacher educators in the FE sector. Similarities were ascertained concerning social constructions, emotional connections, student–teacher identities, and tacit pedagogies. Analysed differences included (1) policies, politics, and institutions, and (2) modelling, research, and profession under construction. However, there were overlaps in the similarities and differences.

Chapter 5 provided a systematic review of literature rarely employed in the FE sector. Its focus was on teacher educators' knowledge. The identified 52 relevant publications covered the period 2000–2023. The research questions included: (1) To what extent is occupational education (vocational) featured? And (2) What are the overlaps between the education sectors?

Table 5.1 of 20,300 words accompanied this chapter.

The analysis of the 52 publications yielded four headings: description of the studies, theoretical underpinnings, methodology and significant findings. Regarding descriptions, country-based publications were identified, with the US with the most publications. The frequent research topics were knowledge and practice pedagogy. Regarding education disciplines, Mathematics was the highest with 12 mentions, followed by higher education. Theoretical underpinnings focused on knowledge-related studies and followed by pedagogy-related investigations. The two most popular research methods employed by the 52 publications were interviews and questionnaires. Two types of publications were identified: typology and impact. The first related to the classification of the topics researched. The second type concerns effect, influence and understanding of the studies in educational settings. Further sub-types from the two types were delineated.

Regarding the extent of vocationalism, there were five related publications by Duch and Nielsen (2022) (no. 23), Hanley and Thompson (2021) (no. 28), Kidd et al. (2022) (no. 34), Loo (2020) (no. 37), and Thinzarkyaw (2020) (no. 49). They covered coherence education; preparation of teacher educators in the English FE sector; boundary crossing from VET settings to training to teach in FE as teachers, and from FE colleges to universities as teacher educators; 5 publications covering teacher training, pathways, teacher educators' knowledge, their identities, and professional development; and college educators' technological pedagogical content knowledge respectively. Each of these five studies provided differing impacts on the sector and the teacher educator cohort. Concerning education sectors overlaps, commonalities and differences were highlighted.

Implications and Applications

The discussions to date resonate with past policies, reports, and professional standards. The Augar Report (2019) on post-18 education and funding had eight principles. Among them were the beneficiaries of post-18 education, including society, the economy, and individuals; equality of opportunity after the age of 18; reversal of the reduction in numbers in post-18 education; government's responsibility to provide adequate investment; post-18 education could not be entirely reliant on market forces; and post-18 education needed to be forward-looking (Augar 2019). The relevant recommendations included reforming and refunding FE colleges, improving flexibility and lifetime learning, supporting disadvantaged learners, and enhancing the apprenticeship offer. This report also included private training providers. The report's principles chimed with the four FE characteristics and social justice established in this monograph. Extra funding in 16–19 settings was available in October 2019 (DfE 2019) to recover from learning lost in the COVID-19 lockdowns (and not resulting from the recommendation of the Augar Report). The White Paper (DfE 2021), Skills for Jobs, focused on post-16 skills, apprenticeships, T Levels (to levels 4 and 5), and support of outstanding teaching, including 'a high-quality apprenticeships teaching workforce'.

Chapters 2–5 of the monograph are relevant to the stated aims of the 2021 White Paper. Chapter 2 on occupational pedagogy will provide critical insights for occupational teachers in apprenticeships and T Levels provisions and supporting outstanding teaching in these programmes. Chapters 3–5 provide a deep understanding of teacher educators to train occupational teachers to deliver the occupational provisions in the 2021 White Paper regarding teacher educators' knowledge and pedagogy (including private providers).

Concerning the touted government work-related provisions of apprenticeships and T Levels in the 2021 White Paper, the former programmes were not responsive to employers' needs, focused on pre-university levels and non-technical areas, but still occupation-based (White Paper 2021), following criticisms in the Richards Review (2012). T Levels were created to address a 'chronic shortage of people with technician skills in the UK' (DfE 2016, p. 7). This approach appears as a sticking-plaster approach. Thus, it is a short-term (solution if so) as the labour market is ever-changeable (Wilde and Loo 2023). T Levels are based on a skills deficit model to benefit the economy along with work placement concerns (NatCen Social Research 2017). Wilde and Loo (2023) found it difficult to see the advantages of T Levels to the well-established and respected BTECs at this early stage.

The final aspect relates to support of outstanding teaching as espoused in the 2021 White Paper. The 1999 Further Education National Training Organization (FENTO) Standards for teaching and supporting learning in further education in England and Wales was a 43-page document specifying teaching standards for the sector. It was not the intention to prescribe the detailed nature of teachers' qualifications. Four values were indicated. They were reflective practice and scholarship, collegiality and collaboration, centrality of learning and learner autonomy, and entitlement, equality, and inclusiveness. The Standards offered three main elements. The listing included professional knowledge and understanding (i.e., domain-wide knowledge, generic knowledge, and knowledge of specific aspects of the standard). The second listing covered personal skills and personal attributes. The third element was eight 'key areas of teaching'. They were assessing learners' needs, planning and preparing teaching, developing pedagogic strategies, managing learning, providing learning support, assessing learning outcomes, reflecting on one's performance, and meeting professional requirements. This 43-page document was the first attempt to professionalise the teacher profession in the sector. Lifelong Learning UK (2007) published the new professional standards for deliverers in the lifelong learning sector and included teacher trainers/educators. Its centrality was on delivering literacy, ESOL and numeracy. This shorter version of 38 pages had six domains. They were professional values and practice, learning and teaching, specialist teaching and learning, planning for learning, assessment, and access and progression. Unlike the 1999 document, this one offered the deliverers, domain descriptions and not listing. Reflection was included on p. 10 for deliverers. Unlike the generic FENTO standards, the LLUK document was specific to the three subjects. The Education and Training Foundation (ETF) published revised professional standards in 2014 in a 9-page document. This reduced document reinforced the notion of teachers and trainers as reflective practitioners. These curtailed standards essentially covered the same elements as the FENTO ones but differently ordered. The new order covered professional values and attributes, professional knowledge and understanding, and professional skills.

The Institute for Apprenticeships and Technical Education (IfATE) (2023) provided the latest version, Learning and Skills Teacher Standard, in September 2023. This 7-page document reframed the Further Education and Skills Sector (FES) teaching as an occupation, and apprenticeships and technical education (T Levels) as central to teaching and learning. There was scant mention of teacher trainers/educators other than working as trainers in large organisations. The list of 'typical job titles' did not include teacher trainers or educators (p. 1). There was a list of nine occupational duties (i.e., passion, outcomes, pedagogy, evidence-informed teaching, diversity, equality and inclusivity, professional relationships with others, and learning support) covering knowledge, skills, and behaviours.

The standards followed the current administration's major push towards apprenticeships and T Levels provisions even though previous government reports and researchers highlighted the inadequacies of the two types of provisions. The focus of FE teaching and learning to work-related provisions provided a reduction and lack of understanding of the diversity and complexity of the sector's roles. Similarly, there was a reduction in the importance of teacher educators and reflective practice. With the latter point, I concur with implementing reflective practice in teacher education and education in general. However, there are fundamental issues, such as an acceptable definition and robust theoretical framework, to address. The four monograph chapters, especially on teacher educators' knowledge and teachers' pedagogies (occupational and academic), etc., would offer stakeholders a welcome ballast to the latest professional standard.

As you can observe above, each of the four standalone chapters offers new insights in their respective ways. Chapter 2 not only proffers a unique conceptual framework of occupational teachers' educational agencies, but it also develops further deeper insights into its relationship with academic discipline delivery. The Mark II framework highlights the complexity of occupational pedagogy (with five recontextualization processes) to academic discipline pedagogy (with three recontextualization processes). Alongside this distinct revelation, the framework subscribes to two more knowledge applications. This refined framework will allow occupational and academic subject deliverers at pre-university, higher education, and professional levels to understand two vital aspects critically. The first refers to the related know-how necessary for their teaching, and the second is the implementation of knowledge in classroom scenarios. In short, this unique framework provides the 'what' and 'how' of occupational and academic subject deliveries.

The findings of Chap. 3 contribute to knowledge about the relatively unknown group of teacher educators in FE. Here, the chapter clarifies the nuanced differences in these educationists' know-how by settings: those in FE colleges, higher education institutions and private trainers. The noteworthy findings impart a profound cognizance of teacher educators' know-how to the related stakeholders. This new understanding, in turn, will enable these educationists, learners, policymakers and curriculum managers to reframe their activities.

Chapter 4 analysis supplies interested parties with unparalleled insight into the relationships between teachers' and teacher educators' knowledge in the sector.

Chapter 5 contributes unmatched perspicacity to teacher educators' knowledge in FE. This chapter is a systematic review of literature; it will be the go-to literature source.

The above findings are used in different ways. Teacher educators (e.g., the Teacher Education in Lifelong Learning (TELL) network) across the teaching institutions in FE colleges, higher education institutions, and private providers may include the pedagogic framework and teachers' knowledge in teacher training programmes. Trainee teachers are the primary beneficiaries (e.g., the Learning and Skills Research Network (LSRN) network). Curriculum managers can utilise this understanding in the curriculum development of teacher education programmes. Awarding bodies such as City and Guilds and related networks (e.g., IfATE) may reflect this new understanding in their specifications and reports. A spin-off of the new knowledge may appear in teacher educators' teaching materials, guidebooks, and textbooks. Regarding new findings (e.g., teacher educators' knowledge and the contrast to teachers' know-how) relating to teacher educators, the apparent beneficiaries are FE teacher educators. They may have a more profound understanding of their roles. The possible spin-offs may result in supportive continuous professional development programmes and career pathways. These educational changes may also be reflected in policymaking and curriculum development. Guidebooks, textbooks, and reports may reflect the findings. And, of course, the new results will serve as significant literature sources for researchers and students in masters, and postgraduate research programmes. Finally, academic libraries will require to stock this monograph for their academic users, especially in countries like the US, Canada, the UK, Europe, Australia, and New Zealand, as with the other eight books.

Conclusion and Directions for Further Research

The four standalone chapters on the Mark II theoretical framework of the occupational pedagogies of teachers, the occupational education of teacher educators' knowledge and pedagogy in three teaching settings of FE colleges, universities, and private providers, the professional identities of English teachers, and teacher educators in the FE sector, and the systematic review of literature of teacher educators' knowledge provided deep insights for educating work-focused stakeholders (e.g., learners, lecturers and teacher educators). This monograph also aims to start a debate across the FE, higher education, and professional education sectors. These deep understandings would facilitate learners joining the economic workforce. In short, this book, a collection of standalone contributions, offers a beachhead around which new studies and research can cluster.[1]

Regarding possible areas of research, these might be viewed as micro, meso and macro levels. The micro level relates to the stakeholders especially the lecturers, teacher educators and learners with emphasis on what do they do perspectives. The related research areas might cover occupational roles, duties of teachers and teacher educators, related identities, teacher training/education, knowledge, pedagogy, student outcomes/achievements and progression, etc. The meso level covers institutions, such as FE colleges, FE/HE institutions, and beyond remembering the porosity of this sector. The emphasis is on how to support teaching and learning activities and the related agencies. Some areas of research might include continuous professional development for the related occupational staff, recognition of formal accreditation and pathways to teaching (such as lecturers and teacher educators), and trainee staff in teaching and support functionalities. The macro level entails national and transnational agencies, whether they are government-related or not. The emphasis is on which policies best support the relevant sector(s). Some research areas include policymaking, diversity, pathways for occupational and academic deliverers, recognition of the sector and its staff, professional standards, funding, and connection with other sectors, education systems, relations with technological advances including online pedagogies and simulation-based occupational deliveries, and sectoral impact to work and the economy.

References

Augar P (2019) Independent panel report to the Review of Post-18 Education and Training. Her Majesty's Stationery Office, London
Bourdieu P (1992) Logic of practice. Polity Press, Bristol
Department for Education (2016) Post-16 skills plan. https://assets.publishing.service.gov.uk/government/uploads/system/uploads/attachment_data/file/536043/Post-16_Skills_Plan.pdf
Department for Education (2019) All schools and colleges to receive extra funding for catch up. Department for Education, London. https://www.gov.uk/government/news/all-schools-and-colleges-to-receive-extra-funding-for-catch-up
Department for Education (2021) Skills for jobs: lifelong learning for opportunity and growth. Her Majesty's Stationery Office, London
Duch H, Nielsen BL (2022) Stakeholder perspectives on vocational teacher education and teacher educators role in supporting coherence. In: Loo S (ed) Teacher educators in vocational and further education. Springer, Cham, Switzerland
Education and Training Foundation (ETF) (2014) Professional standards for teachers and trainers in education and training. ETF, London

---

[1] I am grateful to the Reviewer's suggestion.

Evans K (2016) Higher vocational learning and knowledgeable practice: the newly qualified practitioner at work. In: Loo S, Jameson J (eds) Vocationalism in further and higher education: policy, programmes and pedagogy. Routledge, Abingdon

Further Education National Training Organization (FENTO) (1999) Standards for teaching and supporting learning in further education in England and Wales. FENTO

Hanley P, Thompson R (2021) 'Generic pedagogy is not enough': teacher educators and specialist pedagogy in the Further Education and Skills sector in England. Teach Teach Educ 98:103233

Institute for Apprenticeships and Technical Education (IfATE) (2023) Learning and Skills Teacher Standard. IfATE, London

Kahneman D (2012) Thinking, fast and slow. Penguin Books, London

Kemmis RB, Green A (2013) Vocational education and training teachers' conceptions of their pedagogy. Int J Training Res 11(2):101–121. https://doi.org/10.5172/ijtr.2013.11.2.101

Kidd W, Viswarajan S, McMahon A (2022) Reflexivity for whom? The ethics of a craft identity and the know-how of supporting reflexivity on teacher education programme. In Loo S (ed) Teacher educators in vocational and further education. Springer, Cham, Switzerland

Lifelong Learning UK (LLUK) (2007) New overarching professional standards for teachers, tutors and trainers in the lifelong learning sector. LLUK, London

Loo S (2012) The application of pedagogic knowledge to teaching: a conceptual framework. Int J Lifelong Learn 31(6):705–723

Loo S (2014) Placing 'knowledge' in teacher education in the English further education teaching sector: an alternative approach based on collaborative and evidence-based research. Br J Educ Stud 62(3):337–354

Loo S (2018) Teachers and teaching in vocational and professional education. Routledge, Abingdon

Loo S (2020) Professional development of teacher educators in further education: pathways, knowledge, identities, and vocationalism. Routledge, Abingdon

NatCen Social Research (2017) Work experience and work placements. https://natcen.ac.uk/our-research/research/work-experience-and-work-placements/

Shulman LS (2005) The signature pedagogies of the professions of law, medicine, engineering, and the clergy: potential lessons for the education of teachers. In: The math science partnerships workshop: "teacher education for effective teaching and learning", National Research Council's Centre for Education, Irvine, California, US, 6–8 Feb

The Richard Review of Apprenticeships (2012). https://assets.publishing.service.gov.uk/government/uploads/system/uploads/attachment_data/file/34708/richard-review-full.pdf

Thinzarkyaw W (2020) The practice of technological pedagogical content knowledge of teacher educators in education colleges in Myanmar. Contemp Educ Technol 11(2):159–176

Wilde J, Loo S (2023) VET in FE: T levels and BTEC programmes. FE News. https://www.fenews.co.uk/exclusive/vet-in-fe-t-levels-and-btec-programmes/. Accessed: 16 Feb 2023

Printed in the USA
CPSIA information can be obtained
at www.ICGtesting.com
CBHW070735160924
14542CB00003B/98